YOUNG PEOPLE + MISSION

A PRACTICAL GUIDE

EDITED BY ALISON AND DAVID BOOKER

CHURCH HOUSE
PUBLISHING

Church House Publishing
Church House
Great Smith Street
London SW1P 3NZ

Tel: 020 7898 1451
Fax: 020 7898 1449

ISBN 978–0–7151–4060–4

Published 2007 by Church House Publishing

The opinions expressed in this book are those of the authors and do
not necessarily reflect the official policy of the General Synod of
The Archbishops' Council of the Church of England.

Typeset by RefineCatch Limited, Bungay, Suffolk
Printed in England by The Cromwell Press Ltd, Trowbridge, Wiltshire

YOUNG PEOPLE + MISSION

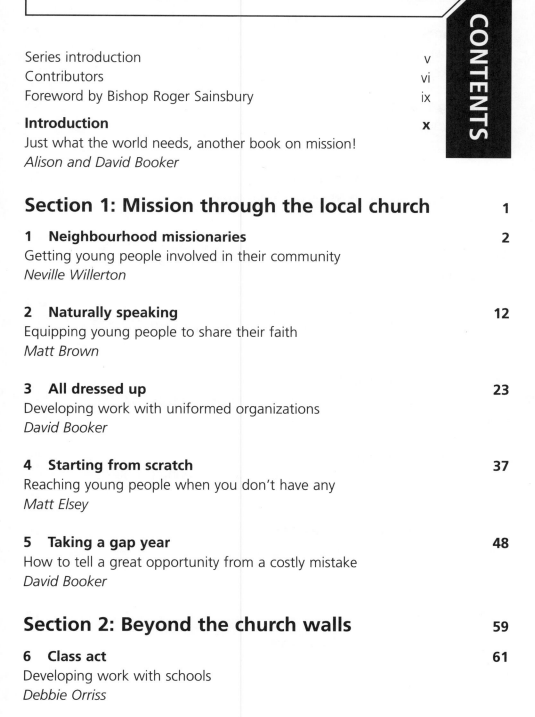

CONTENTS

SERIES INTRODUCTION

This title is one of a series commissioned by Church House Publishing to explore further the themes of the Church of England's National Youth Strategy, which is entitled 'Good news for young people' (downloadable from www.cofe.anglican.org/info/education/youth/youthstrategytwo.pdf). The strategy has four main themes: young people and mission, young people and worship, young people as leaders, and resourcing youth workers.

These titles are aimed at youth workers and leaders, whether paid or voluntary, and at youth workers in training on the increasing number of professional and degree courses in youth work and ministry. Church leaders and members with an interest in developing their church's work with young people will also find them helpful.

Contributors to each title are experienced practitioners in their field. Each volume offers a mixture of practical tips, reflection, real-life case studies and advice on taking things further. The experiences shared and wisdom offered here are intended to be starting points to stimulate your own thinking and practice, as applied to the situation in which you work.

It is our hope that you will find much here to inspire, and challenge, your work with young people.

YOUNG PEOPLE + MISSION

Alison Booker (Editor) is currently the Assistant Minister in a large parish, working across a wide range of ages including children and young people. She has a wide range of experience, including supporting young adults taking gap years, editing Bible notes and research in the area of emerging church. Alison loves a challenge and in her spare time has climbed Ben Nevis and Snowdon (from the lowest starting point) but still has her eyes on Everest!

David Booker (Editor)   Over the last 13 years David has worked in local church, diocesan and national posts with young people and their leaders. In 2000 he launched www.word-on-the-web.co.uk, a project that delivers daily bible readings by email to around 10,000 users. Until 2005 David was Youth Ministry Adviser for the Diocese of Leicester, where he still lives. He is now studying and developing a number of writing projects as well as a love for Shakespeare.

Matt Brown has been involved in full time youth ministry for twelve years in a variety of settings. He is currently director of the Reality Youth Project and is passionate about evangelism, discipleship and training young people to become multiplying disciples of Christ.

Helen Dearnley trained for ministry at Westcott House Cambridge. When not scuba diving, or camping, she can be found serving at Her Majesty's pleasure, working as Coordinating Chaplain in a prison where a high percentage of the prisoners are under 25, a stark contrast to the leafy suburban parish where she served her curacy.

Matt Elsey has been involved in the Salvation Army all his life. He was a key player in preparing for the relocation of the Leicester Castle corps to south Leicester in 2005. Matt's role was to begin to network and build relationships in an area where the Salvation Army had never been involved before. In September 2005 he commenced his study to become an Officer (minister) in the Salvation Army.

Diana Greenfield has been in full-time Christian ministry with Church Army since 2000. She has been a clubber for much longer, with her formative time in club ministry spent serving as a volunteer on the Norwich Youth for Christ team. Currently working in Maidstone, Diana is also studying part time for an MA in theology and contemporary Christianity.

Steve Hollinghurst is Researcher in Evangelism to Post-Christian Culture with a special interest in reaching the increasing majority who don't have church backgrounds. In the past he has been an inner-city youth evangelist and university chaplain and has been part of the UK alternative worship movement since 1990. He has an MA in Postmodernity, the New Age and Paganism in Britain today.

Martyn Lings has a degree in Environmental Management from the University of Manchester and experience in a broad variety of conservation disciplines. For the last two years he has been working for A Rocha, initially in Canada and currently in Portugal, where he is assistant to the A Rocha International Director of Science.

Debbie Orriss has been a Church Army officer for nine years, including nearly six years working with children and young people at deanery and parish level. Before that she worked as a primary school teacher and voluntary youth worker. She is currently a tutor and lecturer at Wilson Carlile College of Evangelism in Sheffield.

Martin Parks works for Christian Aid as a youth coordinator based in Bristol, helping youth workers and young people get to grips with global issues. Prior to this he was involved in student and youth work with various local churches.

Nicholas Shepherd spent ten years working for Youth for Christ in Bath and Greenwich and has experience of a wide range of youth work and evangelism. He is currently a stay-at-home Dad, but combines this with study for a doctorate and work as a freelance trainer and writer in youth ministry and mission. He is editor of the *Journal of Youth and Theology* and a series editor for *Youthwork the Resources*.

Neville Willerton is a Church Army officer with a wide experience of working with young people across the UK and Ireland. He speaks at conferences on youth work and mission and launched the Streetreach project, a cross-community servant evangelism project in Belfast. He is currently the minister of a church plant in Shrewsbury.

FOREWORD

As Bishop of Barking, when David Booker was my Mission Officer, I made two speeches on 'Young People and Mission' at General Synod. In 1996 I ended with the challenge – 'A Church that lives for itself will die by itself'. In 2000 I concluded 'I see even greater dangers today of the Church becoming inward-looking and congregational'. Therefore I am delighted to commend this important book with its 'big vision for mission' that is 'outward-looking'.

In The National Youth Agency's 2004–2005 report, 'The voices of young people can make a difference' we stated that, 'One issue that young people have strong views about is the environment and climate change'. I was therefore very pleased, in a book on mission, to read Martyn Lings' chapter on 'Engaging young people in environmental issues'. I was also encouraged by Martin Parks' call for young people 'to be prophetic and speak up for those whose voice has been gagged' (which echoes the call of a recent Centre for Youth Ministry booklet, Young People as Prophets (Grove Books, 2006)).

Youth work today also has to take seriously the fact that we live in a multi-faith society. David Booker does this for Christian youth work in chapter 8 when he says 'Authentic Christian mission involves a call to love, serve and witness to the whole world, including those of other faith communities. If our love for others does not overcome our suspicion, racism and fear we will never equip our young people to fulfil their call to mission.' I have found the 'Parable of the Good Samaritan' (Luke 10.25-37) a mission challenge that is very relevant for young people in our multi-faith society.

This is an exciting practical book, written by authors who all have a rich variety of experience, with a challenging conclusion – 'With so many opportunities and needs in the lives of young people, what are we waiting for?'

Bishop Roger Sainsbury
Chair of The National Youth Agency and the Centre for Youth Ministry

INTRODUCTION

Just what the world needs, another book on mission!

Alison and David Booker

What do we mean by 'mission'?

Mission is one of those words we are very used to hearing in the Church. However, if you were to ask ten Christians who work with young people about their understanding of mission, you would probably get at least eleven answers! Mission is a word that delights some and sends others running in panic, depending on what it conjures up in their mind.

A shorthand definition might be that our mission as Christians is to work with God in building his kingdom. However, while theologically correct, that definition needs some unpacking if we are really to get to grips not only with what we mean by the word mission, but also with what we should be doing about it.

Jesus and mission

John 10.10 records Jesus telling his disciples he had come to bring 'life in all its fullness'. Jesus draws out the implications of this fullness of life (which Luke records in his gospel) in a passage often known as the Kingdom Manifesto:

> The Spirit of the Lord is on me,
> because he has anointed me
> to preach good news to the poor.
> He has sent me to proclaim freedom for the prisoners
> and recovery of sight for the blind,
> to release the oppressed,
> to proclaim the year of the Lord's favour.
>
> Luke 4.18-19 (NIV)

Jesus, then, comes to set people free from all that holds them back, so that they are able to experience all the fullness of life that God has in store for them. He comes to allow all humanity to reach the potential that God lovingly planted in them. The ministry of Jesus shows us mission in action as lives are made whole and God's kingdom is established. This means that mission is not simply some bright idea the Church has invented and taken on itself to do; rather, God invites us to join in with the mission of reconciling the world to himself. God is already labouring in his world; the privilege and responsibility we have as Christians is to be invited to join in God's mission, as co-workers.

Why do mission?

Knowing we are co-workers with God in mission should give us a great sense of excitement. Excitement because God calls us as co-workers not because he has to, but because he has actively chosen to work in cooperation with us. This perspective – of being chosen by God and invited to join in – changes mission from a demand about which we can so easily feel guilty to a wonderful gift we are requested to share. It means that the answer to the question 'Why do we do mission?' is not so much because the Bible tells us to, or because people have needs, although both of these answers are true. The real answer to why we do mission is because God does not want to build up his kingdom on his

> 'The real answer to why we do mission is because God does not want to build up his kingdom on his own. We do mission because God desires to do mission with us. And if God invites us who are we to say no?!'

own. We do mission because God desires to do mission with us. And if God invites us, who are we to say no?!

One key definition of what we mean by mission, which has now been broadly taken up across the Church, was laid out by the 1988 Lambeth Conference. The conference identified five areas, or marks, of mission activity to which the Church is called.

1. To proclaim the news of the kingdom.
2. To teach, baptize and nurture new believers.
3. To respond to human needs by loving service.
4. To seek to transform unjust structures of society.
5. To strive to safeguard the integrity of creation, to sustain and renew the life of the earth.

Quite an intimidating list of what we the Church are called to do! No wonder when some people hear the word mission they want to throw their hands up and run away. However, while the Church as a body is called to this wide range of tasks, inevitably any individual reading this list will find themselves more excited about one or two areas than the others. Some Christians naturally find themselves concerned about injustice while others are strongly motivated to see people come to faith. Some are naturally pastoral and will want to see new Christians grow, while others will feel a great concern for God's creation.

EVANGIMISSION, or how to mistake mission to and with young people for evangelism

Too often we (those of us who work with young people included) see mission through the narrow lens of the Lambeth Conference mark that we are most concerned about or comfortable with. Ignoring the other marks, we emphasize only the one that comes most naturally to us, and expect everyone else to be as concerned about it as we are. We can even sometimes question the Christian commitment of others who fail to share our concern for our particular favourite mark. There is a constant danger that we reduce mission down to only one of its parts rather than being able to see it in the whole.

At the risk of offending many friends and fellow evangelists, I would argue that often those in the greatest danger of reducing mission to only one of its component parts are those whose focus is on proclaiming the good news of the kingdom. Some parts of the Church do use the words mission and evangelism interchangeably; for example, for many Christians a mission is the name for a week of special events designed to bring people to faith. Another example of this confusion is the number of books that claim to be about young people and mission but are really only about converting young people to the Christian faith. Evangelism is one particular and crucial aspect of the mission God calls us to share, but it is only a part.

Evangelism, sharing the faith with others in a way that challenges them to make their own response to Christ, is a high calling. I passionately want to see young people come to a personal living faith in Jesus Christ. However, this is not all I believe God wants for them. Rather, he wants them to go on and live the kind of lives he created them for, free of the things that hold them back and stop them being who they could be. The danger in so much current Church based youth work is that it is focused only on bringing young people to faith. In this model, youth ministry success and failure is seen simply in the numbers who 'make a commitment', when in reality we are called to so much more.

Simply equating mission with conversion fails to take seriously the breadth of God's concern and care for his creation; it damages our understanding because it reduces Christianity down to a personal choice with no implications for how we treat our neighbour. Secondly, rather than valuing the different concerns God gives his people, it implicitly tells those who find themselves passionate about other areas of mission that they are second-rate Christians who really ought to be more committed.

However, the other extreme is also present in the Church's work with young people. There are those who believe that any attempt to share faith is intrinsically wrong because it involves them telling young people how they should think. Some youth workers understand their role as enabling young people on their journey and see no need to offer them Christianity as an option they should consider. For them any attempt to convert young people implies manipulation of the vulnerable and is basic bad practice.

Most of the time these two approaches to understanding mission keep out of each other's way. They have their own networks, conferences and resources and so never have to interact with each other in a meaningful way. However, if those who work with young people want to engage in the fullness of God's call to mission, such a divide will not do. We are called to invite young people to share our faith in Christ and we are also called to meet their needs and help them live in the fullness God intended. Focusing on just one side or the other of this equation simply sells young people short and gives them a false picture of what God is concerned about. Limiting mission to only our particular passion presents a small vision of God's concerns. A big vision of mission in all its fullness will inevitably be more attractive than a narrow vision for mission that has room only for young people with a certain set of skills or concerns.

> 'We are called to invite young people to share our faith in Christ and we are also called to meet their needs and help them live in the fullness God intended.'

A range of perspectives

This book seeks in its chapters to learn from those on both sides of the divide and provide a broad overview of the mission to which we are called. Having a broad range of writers means that as you read through the book some chapters may appear too theologically narrow and others too 'liberal' in the way they present their ideas. Editing the chapters, we have tried to help the writers to clarify their thinking and expression but have tried not to smooth out these differences of perspective. While we all tend to believe we are perfectly balanced and other people are biased to one extreme or the other, we need to listen and hear those whose outlook on mission is different from ours. Each of the writers in their chapter is expressing their thoughts about an area of mission close to their heart. Listening is the key to successful mission but if we are too proud to listen to our brothers and sisters in the Church who have different perspectives, how will we ever manage to listen to the world? If you find yourself frustrated by the perspective of a particular contributor it may be worth asking yourself why, and whether the frustration is because they are exploring an area that, although not natural to you, is one you should be examining more closely.

> 'A truly mission-focused ministry is actually more likely to attract new members than one narrowly focused on conversion.'

The content of the book has been chosen in the belief that a church or youth ministry that takes mission seriously, in all its breadth, will be an exciting, challenging and outward looking place that seeks to love and serve the world around. The irony is that a truly mission-focused ministry is actually more likely to attract new members than one narrowly focused on conversion. Why?

Because its outward-looking nature will give it a vitality of life and sense of wholeness that is much more attractive than a lifeboat mentality that seeks only to rescue sinners from the horrors of the world.

In this book you will find chapters exploring how clergy, paid youth workers, volunteers and young people themselves can engage in this broad vision of mission. The writers have been selected because they are people who not only know about their subjects, but also have experience of living them in their daily lives. The principles shared have been learnt through hard work and disappointment as much as by success.

There are of course 101 other issues and opportunities that could have been included in these pages. For example, there is no chapter here that directly focuses on leading young people to faith in a narrow sense, largely because there is so much good material already available. We have also tried to avoid any subjects that are too narrow or that would be relevant only to a few readers. The chapters here discuss the big opportunities and issues we face in working with young people, or that concern young people. Each chapter seeks to raise the questions and inspire further interest rather than claiming to be the final word on its theme. A section of further resources and ideas is included to help those who are motivated to think more about each issue.

There are no shortcuts in youth ministry, no promises that the hard work will always pay off in ways we can see, no escape from being let down and asking ourselves why on earth we keep doing it. Yet the writers gathered here have found an amazing truth. As they step out in mission to and with young people, they discover again and again that God has beaten them to it. God has already been working and is ready to meet and surprise them in the work they do with young people.

How to use this book

The book falls into three broad sections.

SECTION 1: Mission through the local church

The chapters in this section look at issues relevant to any youth leader in the work they are doing. They focus on the work of the local church and its young people in mission, giving practical information and advice about getting on with the job of mission.

SECTION 2: Beyond the church walls

The second section encourages leaders to look beyond the church, beyond the immediate opportunities and needs of their young people and towards the needs of their neighbours. These chapters challenge us to move beyond the comfortable youth work boundaries we so easily create, towards a broader vision of the implications of God's mission.

SECTION 3: Rethinking young people and mission

The final section is more reflective. These chapters seek to raise questions about why and how we do what we do. What are the assumptions behind what we do and what are the factors that make our work seem successful or not? Youth workers tend to be activists rather than reflecting on their work, but if we are to keep youth mission relevant we need the space to think about how what we do relates to the culture in which we and the young people we work with live. These chapters challenge assumptions and raise important questions; they do not, however, provide any easy answers. Mind you, if you had wanted another book full of '10 ways to have a successful youth ministry in a fortnight' you would have already put this one back on the shelf.

> **'If we are to keep youth mission relevant we need the space to think about how what we do relates to the culture in which we and the young people we work with live.'**

Chapter sections

Each chapter is split into a number of sections. The *introduction*, not surprisingly, does exactly what it implies, introduces the theme of the chapter. *The issue* section explores the issue and why the theme of the chapter matters to our understanding of young people and mission. The *background/theological* section then gives an understanding of what is really involved and the theological basis for our understanding. A *need to know* section gives practical understanding and a *case study* seeks to put the theme into a context that shows how it works in practice. Finally, a *thinking it through* section has questions for reflection, mostly aimed at youth leaders themselves, but sometimes also relevant to the young people we work with. A youth leadership team could perhaps use this section to think through one of the issues raised in the book and how it could impact their ongoing programme. Each chapter ends with a short *summary* and a *taking it further* list of resources, books, websites and organizations that work in this area, so that the issues raised here can be explored more fully. These organizations cover a broad spectrum of work and not all are Christian. Their inclusion should not be seen as an endorsement of all the attitudes or views they present. Some are aligned to particular parts of the Church and will suit those within that stream but not those outside it. Just as these chapters form a starting point for exploring issues, the *taking it further* sections are also a starting point, not a comprehensive list of groups engaged in each area. If your favourite group for resourcing a particular issue is not listed, we can only apologize!

A note on terminology

Throughout the book the terms youth leader and youth worker are used interchangeably and do not assume that the leader or worker is paid for their role. Where an issue is particularly relevant for a paid worker that point is clearly made in the text.

Being called by God to share his mission is both exciting and humbling. There are times of joy and times of disappointment, of frustration and of wonder. We hope as you read these pages that you will be inspired, reassured and challenged to try and keep up with God. Accepting the invitation of being involved in mission with and to young people is an amazing adventure. God is already at work: our task is to recognize God's action and keep in step.

Alison and David Booker
September 2006

MISSION THROUGH THE LOCAL CHURCH

The first section of this book explores areas that are within reach of anyone seeking to work with young people in a local church. They aim to help readers say 'Hey, we could do that!' and recognize the opportunities that are often already staring them in the face.

The first two chapters focus on inspiring young people to do things for themselves rather than seeing them as the recipients of ministry. Neville Willerton, a Church Army evangelist with experience of working in both England and Northern Ireland, explores what is involved in getting young people active in mission in their own areas. Then Matt Brown, Director of the Reality Youth Project, who spends his time in local church- and schools-based ministry, shares ways of equipping young people to share their faith with their peers.

Having looked at mission with young people we then look at how a youth leader or minister can develop new areas of contact with young people. Salvation Army youth and community worker Matt Elsey shares his story of developing a work with young people from scratch and the principles he has learned in the process.

The first section closes with a chapter designed to help those who work with young people thinking about gap year opportunities. A gap year can, at best, be a great opportunity to be involved in the reality of mission. At worst it can be a costly and disillusioning experience. The chapter aims to resource leaders in helping their young people tell the difference.

Underlying all of these chapters is the belief that youth work is a long-term process rather than a quick-fix solution and that its effectiveness is based on the relationships built between leaders and young people rather than clever ideas and well-resourced programmes. Each writer has known disappointment as well as the joys of success. They set out to show that developing mission to and with young people is tough but possible, and well worth the effort.

1 NEIGHBOURHOOD MISSIONARIES: Getting young people involved in their community

Neville Willerton

INTRODUCTION: Young people doing mission . . .

One of the most disturbing ways in which young people become marginalized is through having too much done for them. Sadly, this can be especially true within the Church. However, the model we see in the Gospels is of Jesus releasing his young disciples into responsible places of mission, an interesting model for church and youth ministry! Jesus did this at huge risk to his own credibility. Young people have so much to give and lots of passion to go with it. Any youth ministry that can release young people to be responsible for their own faith and mission is going to be crucially important to the future of the Church.

THE ISSUE: Not doing mission for young people

Recently there has been a thrilling emergence of serving mission projects developing throughout the UK. Large-scale examples include among others Soul in the City in London, Streetreach in Belfast, Soul Purpose in Shrewsbury, and Festival Manchester. These initiatives have taken literally thousands of young missionaries on to the streets of our towns and cities seeking to give a practical demonstration of the love of Christ. (An examination of the 'tourist' aspect of these missions can be found in Nick Shepherd's chapter in the final part of this book.) Emerging from this large-scale movement has been a new discovery in many local youth groups of service as an act of mission.

> 'Recently there has been a thrilling emergence of serving mission projects developing throughout the UK ... These initiatives have taken literally thousands of young missionaries on to the streets of our towns and cities seeking to give a practical demonstration of the love of Christ.'

One of these initiatives has been Streetreach in Belfast, a project founded by Summer Madness, Ireland's largest Christian festival. Over the last four years this initiative has been developed to bring young Catholics and Protestants together to serve their communities. Streetreach is a fantastic opportunity to build bridges across communities and denominations, especially at 'sensitive' times of the year in Northern Ireland. A Catholic youth worker who was very involved with the project commented on the success of the mission:

> Young Catholics and Protestants being Christians together, united in a way that made Christ's love, not difference of doctrine, central. This was real Church – with mission at its core!

One of the team leaders who shared her experience in the Lower Falls area of Belfast during Streetreach said:

> At the start of the week a local child told me he hated me because I was a Protestant. However, later on in the mission he asked to shake my hand and said he no longer cared what denomination I was because he liked me.

Not only were streets transformed but lives too!

Many events took place throughout Streetreach, including paramilitary paintings taken down, kids' clubs, a multi-cultural street picnic, and a huge party in a local park with bouncy castles, BBQs and face painting which attracted over 1,000 local people. At a personal level a single mother who had eight children obviously didn't have much time for her garden, which was high with weeds and rubbish. The Streetreach team worked there throughout the week clearing the rubbish, levelling the soil and laying turf. Finally they left the family with the gift of a play swing. These are some of the effects that young people serving their community can have.

THE THEORY: Mission on the street

I once spent a few days at a series of meetings on church growth. There was one particular meeting where I drifted into the back, not really engaging with what was being said from the front. I picked up my Bible and began reading through the first ten chapters of Mark's Gospel (it was a very long meeting!). Two things struck me as I read. Every chapter and every paragraph was about

> **'Jesus taught his disciples about mission out in the community, in the market place, on the hillside, by the beach, anywhere people congregated, that was "their turf".'**

mission. For instance, it records Jesus telling the story about the yeast in the dough (a story about mission), appointing a few fisherman to be his disciples and follow him (to help him in mission), feeding over 5,000 people (a mission barbecue!), and a healing mission. During these chapters, Christ also sent out the disciples (on mission) – I could go on. The second thing that struck me was that every single instance recorded here took place outside; it was never in a church/synagogue meeting place. Jesus taught his disciples about mission out in the community, in the market place, on the hillside, by the beach, anywhere people congregated, that was 'their turf'.

The vision of servant mission and evangelism is to serve our communities and engage them with the love of Christ. These are exciting days to live in because God seems to be raising up a generation of radical young worshippers whose desire is to serve him and the world in which they live. Through radical mission initiatives such as 'The Noise', 'Soul in the City', 'Festival Manchester' and 'Soul Purpose' this emphasis on serving mission is really catching hold of young people's imagination.

James lived in a town south of Belfast and the people around him noticed a change in his attitude throughout the few days that a mission was operating there. At first he was abusive to one of the young people doing the mission, kicking him and spitting on his jacket before asking 'What are you going to do now?' The young missioner replied by saying, 'I am going to carry on serving this area and weeding this garden.' In time, James started to weed the garden as well and a barrier between the two was broken down. On the last night at an evening concert in the local high school, James came along and sat at the front enjoying the music and the message. During the event he gave his life to Christ and it was the young person he had been abusive to that prayed for him and led him to Christ. The opportunity that we have before us in releasing young people in mission is immense.

There are two 'Greats' in the Bible. The first is the 'Great Commandment', which goes like this: ' "Love the Lord your God with all your heart and with all your soul and with all your mind." This is the first and greatest commandment. And the second is like it: "Love your neighbour as yourself" '(Matthew 22.37-39). Servant evangelism, I believe, encapsulates this. The second 'great' is the Great Commission, where Jesus appears to his disciples and breathes on them the Holy Spirit and says 'All authority in heaven and earth has been given to me. Therefore go and make disciples of all nations' (Matthew 28.18-19). That is a huge encouragement for us, to realize the authority that Christ has given us.

I pray that the serving hands and praying hearts of young people will change this country and turn hearts back to Christ. Jesus Christ has a heart to impact our communities with his love and he has chosen his Church to be a part of that. The key principle is not to preach condemnation or turn people away from Christ, as so often seems to happen in evangelism. The heart of mission is to show a practical demonstration to local communities that God cares for people's everyday lives. One of the best ways to do that is by painting a fence, picking up rubbish, weeding a garden, giving flowering tubs away, or running a children's club.

> 'The heart of mission is to show a practical demonstration to local communities that God cares for people's everyday lives.'

NEED TO KNOW: Finding how you can serve

If you feel inspired and want to take things further with your young people, you should perhaps put together a serving mission with them for your area. One of the main keys to a successful outreach is identifying the 'real' needs within your area. Given that your young people already live there, they will have a pretty good idea what needs to be done, but you could also spend some time going out and asking people how they feel about the community they live in and what would improve it. In setting up the project you need to ensure that it has a high visibility and impact in the area. You need to communicate with local people so that it is effective in representing the needs of the community and picks up the feel of the area. Listed below are some possible ideas for a serving mission, many of which I have already used. They can help your outreach to have a massive impact in your area and transform the way people see the Church:

- Free car wash
- Free jumble sale – give things away and see the impact it has!
- Giving away flowering tubs/hanging baskets
- A picnic for refugees
- A trip for senior citizens
- Painting a fence
- Lifting rubbish (in gardens and community areas)
- Weeding a garden
- Painting a youth centre/house/community centre
- Shoe shine
- Free beautician treatment (nail bar, hairdressing, facials)
- An evening concert
- A family fun night (bouncy castles, games etc.)
- A free barbecue
- Balloon giveaway
- Painting out graffiti
- Service in an old people's home – either helping out practically, or leading a worship service
- Putting on a meal/entertainment evening for the community
- Games with local kids
- Street café
- Street party
- Coffee/tea/canned drinks giveaway
- Doughnut giveaway
- Birthday or Christmas present wrapping service
- Children's face painting

If you have a good imagination and a love for your community then the list could well be endless . . .

I have found it a great benefit in these mission projects to encourage young people from different denominations to serve on mission together. Also to stretch our thinking, I have done practical mission projects and had people on the team who don't express a faith. This has proved a massive benefit in 'rubbing shoulders' with and ministering alongside people of no faith background, in making good relationships and learning from ways that 'outsiders' consider the Church. Maybe that is a lot for people to consider, but it may help to look at the spiritual state of all the disciples that Jesus took on mission? After all, Christ knew the spiritual state of Judas and yet still took him on mission. An interesting thought, isn't it, and one that prevents us thinking we have to be perfect before we start!

CASE STUDY: Why words are not enough

When I trained for the ministry I spent four weeks in London working with several churches. The last week of the placement was a mission with the local churches of that particular community. As I was walking across the town I noticed a group of about ten lads with whom I had had some contact throughout my time in the area. I approached them and, once we got chatting, invited them along to the final event of the mission to be held in one of the participant churches. I went on to the event and part way through the young lads walked in and sat themselves down at the rear of the meeting room.

As the evening progressed, I noticed that the people at the front were getting increasingly agitated by the young people at the back. At one point, after the speaker had concluded, the leader invited questions. Consequently, things seemed to improve within the meeting. Then beside me a young lad shot up his hand and blurted out a question, which was something like 'How do you get to know God?' I thought 'Wow, this is getting really interesting.' However, the guy at the front misheard and mistook the genuine question for more 'dissent' and replied by saying: 'Look lads, this is a serious meeting and you either involve yourselves with what we are doing or there is the door, you either worship with us or you get out.' Unsurprisingly, the young lads walked out and I went with them.

Of course, this story should never have happened and is an indictment of the Church. Interestingly enough, the church that hosted this meeting was not a traditional, centuries-old church; it was one of the 'new churches' perceived by many to be cutting edge. The fundamental error was not just the treatment of the young people within the meeting, although that was bad enough, but the notion that this style of mission, relying only on services, could work in attracting

> **'The Church in mission needs to move from a "come to us" mindset ... to a church that is in the community engaging with what God is doing already.'**

unchurched young people. What I mean is this: the Church in mission needs to move from a 'come to us' mindset, as we were doing with those young people, to a church that is in the community engaging with what God is already doing.

Maybe this is where we can learn from young people and the mission to our communities. I think practical missions are relevant to this context because it is the Church reaching out through serving and not through preaching. It is moving from a negative presumption of telling the world how they need to change, to a positive position of practically serving and meeting needs within the community. It is a missional transition that releases young people into being part of the church's outreach instead of expecting them to conform to passive participation within a church.

THINKING IT THROUGH: Freeing young people to do mission

I believe it is time to think practically and seriously about how we enable our young people in church to put their faith into action. I think it is time that we think seriously and Biblically about mission. How many of our churches have run evangelism or mission courses in the last ten years to train their young people? Not many, I guess. What is good news to a lady living a tough life without a partner and trying to bring up eight kids by herself? What is 'the gospel' in her context? If the Church asks this question of itself honestly and seriously and practically responds in love and care, it has gone a long way to identify itself with those Christ has called it to.

We must ask serious questions about our young people and how they are released into ministry. If we just allow them to lead us in a youth service once a month, good and helpful though this can be, it is only a small part of what young people can do and may suit only those with particular gifts. Are there any young people in my congregation that feel under-utilized or ignored? Is there anything I can do as a church leader to encourage the young people in our community to be recognized and accepted? Maybe a greater focus on community mission would release those young people with gifts that are currently not used?

> **'Are there any young people in my congregation that feel under-utilized or ignored? Is there anything I can do as a church leader to encourage the young people in our community to be recognized and accepted?'**

NEIGHBOURHOOD MISSIONARIES

SUMMARY

We have a real challenge ahead of us to become a church that regains something of the way that Jesus took his church on mission in Galilee. I pray that one day we will catch up with the way Jesus did mission. Jesus loved and accepted people as they were, which is why he is such an attractive figure. Likewise, it is important that we love the whole person and do not just speak and act in terms of a spiritual salvation. Christ addressed the healing of the whole person. What would the Church look like if we operated like Christ? How we respond to young people within our communities and how we do mission are, I believe, issues that are close to the heart of Christ. I know this because he modelled it for us. Is your church or youth group ready to engage in servant mission to its community?

NEIGHBOURHOOD MISSIONARIES

If you want to know more, then *Conspiracy of Kindness* by Steve Sjogren (Vine Books, 1993) is one great place to start.

Internet Resources

The following are some web sites that have inspired and resourced many servant mission projects. Many of these sites are packed with resources and ideas to help you make your mission a massive success.

www.servantevangelism.com

This is a wonderful site full of ideas, resources and examples of the Church out in the streets serving and making Christ known. It is US based.

www.relevantmagazine.com

This is an extensive web site that looks at how our faith can be relevant to the culture and world around us. Prepare to be challenged and provoked. The key sections of the site are God, Life and Progressive Culture.

www.churchnext.net

This web site communicates the Tribal Training network. Some of their stuff on outreach and being church is rather good.

www.churcharmy.org.uk

This evangelistic organization supports StreetReach and other innovative missionary initiatives. Follow the links about what Church Army supports for some good examples.

www.soulsurvivor.com

Follow the links to 'Soul in the City' and 'The Noise', two amazing servant evangelism ('mission') initiatives in the UK.

2 NATURALLY SPEAKING: Equipping young people to share their faith

Matt Brown

INTRODUCTION: Called to witness

When Jesus uttered his last words as recorded in Matthew 28, 'Therefore go and make disciples of all nations', it wasn't just a great idea, it wasn't merely a good suggestion, and it certainly wasn't something you might want to do if you had nothing else planned! What Jesus said on that mountaintop a little over 2,000 years ago to a group of uneducated and scared social outcasts was to change history for ever. Jesus called them to go out and change the world with the good news of the coming of his kingdom. This chapter explores how we can train and inspire Christian young people to engage in the particular mission task of evangelism: that is, sharing the good news in a way that attracts others to respond for themselves.

Too often we forget that what Jesus said to his disciples 2,000 years ago also applies to us today. Surely a key role of those of us who work with young people should be to model ways of sharing faith with those around us and to help and teach our young people to do the same. If we can find a way of training an army of young disciples to share the good news of Jesus, then we might reach our villages, towns and cities for him.

> **'A key role of those of us who work with young people should be to model ways of sharing faith with those around us and to help and teach our young people to do the same.'**

THE ISSUE: Learning to share

A few years ago a 14-year-old lad turned up at a lunchtime group I was running at the local college. Let's call him John. That lunchtime he heard the Christian message for the first time and that very day he made a decision without hesitation to follow Jesus. I arranged to meet up with him the following day just to make sure he had understood what he had done! To my surprise he knew exactly what he had undertaken and for the next two years I had the joy of discipling him and watching him grow in his faith – an awesome experience.

In one of our early discipleship sessions we were talking about sharing our faith with friends. We had a great session talking about the gospel and how everyone in the world needed to hear about it. Very shortly after this I bumped into John in the corridor. He told me how he had been practising sharing his faith. He said that he had been waiting at the bus stop with someone who was well known for being heavily into Wicca. John casually sidled up to him and told him that if he didn't turn to God and away from Wicca he was going to go to hell. Perhaps not surprisingly, John then had to run for his life as his 'target' pursued him. John had a lot to learn about evangelism! I'm pleased to report that his evangelism style is more finely tuned now that he has had some training.

Without a doubt the best people to tell young people about Jesus are other young people. Our job, as adults working with young people, is to train, equip, resource, enable and empower them to do it. Simon Hall, a founder of Revive Church in Leeds, once said, 'For far too long we've been teaching young people to swim in the swimming pool (the safety of the Church), not in the sea (living out their faith in the wider world).' Fortunately, the tide is turning. There is a growing movement of evangelism amongst teenagers in the UK with the birth and rapid growth of events such as Soul in the City. The real question is not, are the young people ready for this, but are we?

> 'Simon Hall, a founder of Revive Church in Leeds, once said, "For far too long we've been teaching young people to swim in the swimming pool (the safety of the Church), not in the sea (living out their faith in the wider world)." '

THEORY: Just how hard can it be?

Before we look at equipping young people to share their faith, we need to look at the issue ourselves. We need to ask ourselves how we define evangelism. How do I feel about it? Am I doing it? Is my church reaching out to people who don't know God? These are big and challenging questions but we must wrestle with them and reflect on them before we embark on this adventure. You've heard it said, 'Don't ask anyone to do something you're not prepared to do yourself.' This is especially true when it comes to sharing your faith. If you are going to ask your young people to step out of their comfort zones, then you need to be willing to lead by example.

So just what is evangelism? There are many definitions, some good, some not so good. I came across one recently that I thought was fantastic. It was actually being used to define discipleship but I think the description is equally true of evangelism: 'Life to life transference of truth'. Evangelism is about investing in someone's life, building a relationship with them, being 'Jesus' to them in what we say and do, and sharing the good news in word and action.

> **'Evangelism is about investing in someone's life, building a relationship with them, being "Jesus" to them in what we say and do, and sharing the good news in word and action.'**

There is a great story in the Old Testament that for me gets to the heart of evangelism. It's the story (told in 2 Kings 7.3-11) of four lepers who find themselves in a bit of a tricky situation. They are at the city gates of Samaria, a city being besieged by the Aramean army. There is a famine in the city. They discuss amongst themselves whether to enter the city – where they will surely die – or to take their chances and surrender to the Aramean army, who might show mercy and spare their lives. They decide to try the latter course of action. However, when they reach the camp of the Aramean army, they find that the Lord has been there already and the army has fled in confusion, leaving everything. The lepers, as I'm sure you can imagine, help themselves to food and drink, silver and gold. Then, in 2 Kings 7.9, they say to each other, 'We're not doing right. This is a day of good news and we are keeping it to ourselves . . . Let's go at once and report this to the royal palace.'

If that's what evangelism is, then how can we do it well? It's said that success in evangelism is simply 'Sharing the good news of Jesus (through word and deed) in the power of the Holy Spirit and leaving the results to God.' Easy! So why do we as God's people have such a problem doing it? Before we can start challenging our young people in this area we need to ensure that we are living, breathing examples of what it means to live out the Great Commission. If we don't do it ourselves, what chance have our young people got?

'Before we can start challenging our young people in this area we need to ensure that we are living, breathing examples of what it means to live out the Great Commission. If we don't do it ourselves, what chance have our young people got?'

There are many reasons why we may have difficulty with 'doing' evangelism and I think that's the heart of the problem. We often see evangelism as something we have to 'do' but actually it should be more about the way we live our lives. Evangelism should be a lifestyle, not just another Christian activity. When we think of evangelism it can often have very negative connotations. We may have had a bad experience in the past, we may naturally be shy and find it difficult to talk to people, or the thought of it may fill us with fear. Whatever the reasons for being hesitant about evangelism, beginning to understand that it is about our lifestyle, not just something we must 'do', will, I think, help us as we seek to challenge ourselves and our young people.

Young people, including those who are Christians, need to see authentic Christian living in action before they will listen to what we have to say.

Evangelism is a life style, not just a teaching programme or something you do at a Friday night youth club. We need to communicate that through what we say to our young people but also and more importantly through how we live our lives. If young people can see that we are willing to build relationships with their friends, to be 'Jesus' to their friends and talk to them about Jesus, in a way that isn't going to make them want to curl up in a corner and die, they are far more likely to think, 'I can do that!'

NEED TO KNOW: Basic skills

So how can we practically equip our young people to begin to share their faith?

We need to start at the beginning and be prepared for this to take a little while. Sharing faith isn't simply a subject for a youth group session every now and then. It is about developing a lifestyle where what we say and how we live match up. It is also about developing young people with the personal confidence to share what they believe with their friends. Young people have to travel on a journey of personal understanding and it won't happen overnight. However, there are significant stepping-stones on the way to learning to share faith with confidence.

We need to make sure that our young people are themselves in a relationship with Jesus

This may sound very obvious, but it is absolutely vital. I heard a story once of a young man doing his gap year, who went on his placement church's youth weekend away. The theme was evangelism and at the end of the weekend he came back distraught because he'd never actually become a Christian himself until that weekend; he had simply gone through the motions of attending church without ever coming to a personal commitment. It can and does happen. We need to ensure that our young people are in a place where they are in a real and growing relationship with God. That way, they will have something genuine to share with others.

We need to teach them what evangelism is and why it's so important

Recently I was asked to lead a youth group session on evangelism at a local church that is very outward looking. I started off by asking the group what they thought evangelism was. Their answers left me speechless and somewhat confused: 'When someone smashes something up', 'When you break something that isn't yours', 'When people graffiti on walls'. So it went on until suddenly the penny dropped – they were actually thinking about vandalism, not evangelism. Even young people who do understand what the word means often have a wrong perception of evangelism. They often see it as standing on a soapbox in the city centre preaching a 'turn or burn' message. We need to change that perception first before we can get much further, and we can do that by teaching a proper biblical understanding of what evangelism actually is and why it's so important. The book *Disciples are Made not Born* by Walter A. Hendrichsen is a good starting point (see resources section). When young people realize how much love God has for their family and friends the passion kicks in and they want to share their faith. Still, passion also needs to be tempered with wisdom if young people are going to be effective in reaching their friends and families rather than annoying them.

> 'Even young people who do understand what the word means often have a wrong perception of evangelism. They often see it as standing on a soapbox in the city centre preaching a "turn or burn" message. We need to change that perception first before we can get much further ...'

We need to teach them to use the tools of the trade

To do any job you need the right tools. The same is true of young people and evangelism. We need to help them understand what the tools of the trade are and how to use them. Not to learn a script that they slavishly follow in all situations, but to feel able to tell their own story of how they became a Christian and what following God means to them. We need to give them confidence to ask questions or drop comments into conversations that may lead on to talking about spiritual things. We need to encourage them to live such radically different lives that people can't help but notice there is something about them. We can help our young people to recognize when they could offer to pray for and with people they know.

> 'We need to help them understand what the tools of the trade are and how to use them. Not to learn a script that they slavishly follow in all situations, but to feel able to tell their own story of how they became a Christian and what following God means to them.'

We should also put on appropriate events, activities and socials to which they can invite their friends. If asked, could we take someone through an outline of the gospel message, explaining God's love and our choice to respond? All of these (and there are many more) are tools of the trade with which we can equip our young people so that they can use the right model in the situations where they find themselves.

We need to give young people structured opportunities to share their faith

It's often down to us as youth leaders to help the young people create an environment to which they can invite non-Christian friends. The possibilities are endless and completely varied. They could include a social trip or a pizza and video evening, sporting occasions or opportunities to serve the community. Working together with your young people so they could put on a 'just looking' type of course such as Youth Alpha, Youth Emmaus or Quest is another way forward. You could either put on or take your young people to a Christian event with a band, to which they can invite their friends. Run a drop-in or even a mission weekend or week in the summer, or take them to one that's happening around the UK or even overseas. Give out free doughnuts at school or in town. Organize visits to local elderly and housebound people. The possibilities are endless, but be prepared for your young people to come up with some crazy ideas. Just remember . . . they know their friends better than you do; by allowing them to shape what happens, it might just work!

Involve young people in the follow up

It may take some time but if your young people really start to understand and put some of these things into practice then they will see people come to faith. It is important that follow-up is in place for these new Christians, either individually or in small groups. It's also really important that we involve our already-Christian young people in this process. Seeing their friends come to Christ and watching them grow will be such a thrill and a real motivator to keep going even when it's tough.

When thing go wrong

Of course things don't always go the way that the young people or we would like them to. So it is really important to give our young people time to talk about frustrations and disappointments as well as celebrating success and achievements. It's also important that our young people know that we are there for them through the bad times and the good, and to keep reminding them that even though we don't always understand, God does and he knows what he's doing.

> 'It is really important to give our young people time to talk about frustrations and disappointments as well as celebrating success and achievements.'

CASE STUDY: ncounter

For a number of years I've led a summer mission called 'ncounter'. It started off as a week of evening drop-ins for local young people. In the first year, by the end of the week we had about 30 young people coming along and had some good conversations with them. The following year we made it into more of a mission and I challenged my young people to come and get trained up in evangelism in the morning, put on evangelistic activities in the afternoon, including sports and film afternoons, and run the drop-in in the evening. We had 14 young people on the team that year and by Wednesday over 100 young people at the drop-in. The following year we had 28 on the team and added an 'emerging leaders' course for those who were on their second ncounter. And last year we had 60 young people on the course in four different bases.

There are so many things that I love about ncounter but one of the most special things is seeing, as we do every year, those young people who come, possibly a little reluctantly, terrified of the thought of sharing their faith. Almost without exception, by days two and three they can't stop telling people about Jesus. One young lady who came on ncounter last year rang me a couple of weeks before, really concerned about coming because she was terrified that she would have to stand up in front of large groups of people and share her faith story. I reassured her that I wouldn't make her do anything she didn't feel comfortable with, but that she would probably find herself doing things that were way out of her comfort zone. She still agreed to come and on Tuesday evening she was found sitting on a grass bank surrounded by a group of young people sharing her testimony with them. That's what ncounter is all about and that's what equipping our young people to share their faith is all about: giving them the confidence to get on and do it!

THINKING IT THROUGH

- How would you define evangelism?
- How important a part of God's wider mission is evangelism to you?
- Are you living an evangelistic lifestyle?
- How is your church doing when it comes to evangelism and how could it give you more support?
- How are your young people doing when it comes to evangelism? Could you plan an event with them to which they could invite their friends?
- How could you integrate the steps mentioned in the 'Need to know' section of this chapter into your youth programme? This may take some time to do but will be hugely beneficial in equipping your young people to share their faith.
- Once you have planned how you might go about equipping your young people, do a SWOT analysis. (Strengths – what are you good at? Weaknesses – what you are not so good at? Opportunities – possibilities for the future. Threats – potential obstacles and stumbling blocks.) It's a useful tool to help you think through the issues involved.
- Are there youth workers, projects or organizations locally that could help you train and equip your young people?

NATURALLY SPEAKING

SUMMARY

I'm going to leave the last words in this chapter to Jonathan Bryant, who wrote a three-part series on 'Youth Evangelism' in *Youthwork* magazine in 2005/2006. When I read this it stirred a passion within me once again to do everything I possibly can to enable my young people to take the gospel into their homes, their schools, their communities and to the four corners of the earth. He writes:

> Evangelism among young people in the UK is vibrant today with a wealth of different styles and ways of gaining a hearing for the Gospel in youth culture. There has been a lot of negative talk recently, in the light of the horrors of suicide bombing, about the radicalization of young people. As ever the devil is merely counterfeiting and seeking to use for evil, death and destruction what God intends for good. Surely the greatest excitement, the greatest challenge is to see a generation of young people rise up 'radicalized' in the best possible sense of the word, to live their lives to bring hope, love, joy, peace and relationship with God to their peers.[1]

NATURALLY SPEAKING

Walter A. Hendrichsen, *Disciples are Made not Born*, Cook Communications, 1988.

The Art of Connecting – a Youth For Christ course on faith sharing skills: www.YFC.co.uk

Youthwork magazine – for resources and articles: www.youthwork.co.uk

Youth Emmaus, Church House Publishing.

Quest (five-week 'just looking' course for young people) www.imagexmedia.com

For Evangelism training resources, also try:
Agape www.agape.org.uk
The Message Trust www.message.org.uk
Youth Alpha www.alphacourse.org

TAKING IT FURTHER

3 ALL DRESSED UP: Developing work with uniformed organizations

David Booker

INTRODUCTION: A missed opportunity?

Take a look around at the adverts for youth worker posts. It seems most of the Church wants a trendy, good looking youth worker who is able to keep up with Cell Church, Alternative Worship, Youth Congregations, Schools work, Youth Alpha, Youth Emmaus, and whatever fashion will come out of the next conference. Amidst all this activity and change it's easy to see uniformed youth organizations as dinosaurs ready for extinction.

Uniformed youth work can seem all too out of place in our postmodern, non-hierarchical, do what you feel culture. However, there is huge, largely untapped, potential for the Church to work well with uniformed groups. Literally tens of thousands of young people are involved in them and many already have strong, if dormant, links with the Church. What follows is an attempt to show how we can unlock this powerful opportunity to work together for the good of young people and learn from the uniformed groups' years of practical experience.

> **'Uniformed youth work can seem all too out of place in our postmodern, non-hierarchical, do what you feel culture. However, there is huge, largely untapped, potential for the Church to work well with uniformed groups.'**

THE ISSUE: Opportunity to serve and learn from those in uniformed youth work

Despite a decline in membership, over one million children and young people under the age of 20 are part of uniformed organizations in the UK. Most

> **'Over one million children and young people under the age of 20 are part of uniformed organizations in the UK.'**

groups are led to a very high standard, with creative and stretching programmes and activities; their leaders are being offered some of the best ongoing training around; and many uniformed groups have leaders who stick around for the long haul in a way that most youth groups can only dream of. What is more, many of these groups are directly linked to the Church in some way, even if many churches do little more than expect them to arrive for church parade. Uniformed groups provide a real opportunity to partner others in mission rather than doing it all ourselves.

Uniformed groups point to a holistic model of working with young people. They are concerned that their members grow in every aspect of their life. For

> **'Uniformed groups point to a holistic model of working with young people. They are concerned that their members grow in every aspect of their life.'**

a church that is often focused only on conversion, they are an important challenge to be broader in our mission. They are often historically rooted in reaching the marginalized and they continue to provide a prophetic voice that youth ministry is needed well beyond the middle class churches who are able to afford a youth worker. Issues of character, leadership and service are part of the culture of uniformed youth organizations. The history of the Boys' Brigade, for example, was as a Christian outreach to boys in the slums of Glasgow. Its founder, Sir William Alexander Smith, saw the need of boys and young men not only to know Christ, but also to be given an education and an opportunity to escape the poverty that held them.

For some young people with chaotic home situations, growing up with few rules and standards, the uniformed group is an important safe place. I have seen that, for some members, the Air Cadets provide a structure to grow in leadership and responsibility; they know what is expected of them and develop the key skill of learning to live within boundaries. It also, of course, opens the window of opportunity to fly a plane, a dream that attracts many members. Large numbers of young people find the structure, discipline and opportunities of uniformed groups far more rewarding and safer than a drop in at the local youth club with its table tennis and tuck shop.

While decline is a threat for many uniformed groups, the decline in numbers has been slower than in more informal forms of church-based youth work. The excellent Boys' Brigade report, *Retention Through the Teenage Years*, makes a point that is valid for all work with young people:

> If the reason for the progressive fall in membership over past years was simply that the organization has refused to adapt or has become out of touch with young people it would be a relatively simple matter to introduce changes to the programme, award scheme, structure and organization together with a high profile publicity campaign in some sort of re-launch and then wait for the numbers to rise again. However, we are located within a complex society which has been through and is still going through rapid social change and so many of the factors affecting what we do are outside our powers to influence. By recognizing the impact of the extraneous factors we can then seek ways of adapting what we do to take them into account.

All youth work needs constantly to ask if it is achieving its aims. What worked for youth leaders when they were young may well not work today, whether it involved wearing a uniform or not. The issues faced by all uniformed groups as they seek to work out their purposes today are really pretty similar to the challenges faced by all youth work. How should we change and adapt to keep on making an effective difference in the lives of young people? There is much the Church can teach and can learn from those in uniform if we take the time to listen to each other. Too often churches run their so-called church youth work totally separate from any uniformed work they have. This is a real loss to both sides!

> 'There is much the Church can teach and can learn from those in uniform if we take the time to listen to each other. Too often churches run their so-called church youth work totally separate from any uniformed work they have. This is a real loss to both sides!'

And not forgetting the role of padres and chaplains!

The military-based uniformed youth organizations all have some kind of a role for a chaplain, although how this works varies from group to group and chaplain to chaplain. For those whose background is youth work and who have no experience of the armed services, these groups can at first seem strangely formal and structured with the use of ranks and titles. However, for those able to work within them such groups provide a unique opportunity to meet the needs of young people.

In my role as chaplain to an Air Training Corps Squadron in Leicester I have had a monthly 'Chaplain's Hour' with the young people. There we can discuss issues the cadets raise, explore moral or ethical dilemmas, or spend time looking at what Christians believe and why. My role there is not to force them to believe, but I do have a clear opportunity to help the cadets think for themselves and explore the Christian life and way of seeing the world. At the same time there is the opportunity for a pastoral role with the young people and staff, many of whom may not meet with a minister in any other setting than their group. There is a real need for sensitive people who are willing to take up the role of a chaplain and the Church really should not miss this opportunity.

BACKGROUND: A rough 'who's who' of uniformed youth work

The Boys' Brigade

Founded in 1882, the BB was the first Christian uniformed organization for boys in the world and today has around 100,000 members in the UK. A local church sponsors each of the more than 2,000 companies. The following extract is taken from the BB report *Retention Through the Teenage Years*:

> Our primary task is not simply to entertain boys and young men but to assist their personal and social development and, above all, to bring them within the influence of Christian adults who are committed to ensuring they receive sound Christian teaching and receive the challenge of the gospel of Jesus Christ. Whether or not a boy makes a personal commitment to Jesus Christ is a matter for him alone.

The Girls' Brigade

The stated aim of the Girls' Brigade is 'To help girls to become followers of the Lord Jesus Christ and through self control, reverence and a sense of responsibility to find true enrichment of life.' Like the BB each company is linked to a local church. It has contact with around 30,000 children and young people each week.

The Church Lads' and Church Girls' Brigade

The Church Lads' and Church Girls' Brigade is an exclusively Anglican uniformed youth organization. Its object is 'to extend the Kingdom of Christ among Lads and Girls and to encourage faithful membership of the Church'. The web site of the Brigade goes on to explain: 'Worship and Christian teaching at Section meetings, which help children respond to God's love for them is a vital part of the programme.'

The Scouts

With 500,000 members, the Scout Association is the largest mixed youth movement in the United Kingdom. Scouting provides activities and personal development opportunities in over 8,000 groups throughout the country. Scouting encourages members 'to develop confidence, independence, integrity and a spirit for adventure'. Some groups have a formal church sponsor, others do not.

Girlguiding UK

Girlguiding UK has around 600,000 children and young people in membership. Its web site gives the following as its mission and vision:

Girlguiding UK enables girls and young women to fulfil their potential and to take an active and responsible role in society through its distinctive, stimulating and enjoyable programme of activities delivered by trained volunteer leaders.

Armed Services-linked uniformed youth work

Each local unit of Armed Services-linked group has a chaplain to support it and lead sessions with the young people. Church parade is also a regular part of many programmes, particularly for special occasions such as Remembrance Sunday and Battle of Britain Sunday.

Air Cadets

The web site of the Air Cadets (ATC) begins with this introduction to the organization:

> Cadets in your local Air Training Corps (ATC) and Combined Cadet Force (CCF(RAF)) are enjoying flying, gliding, going on camps, taking part in all kinds of action, adventure and sports. It's great fun too, with the opportunity to enjoy an enviable social life and make many new friends. How far are YOU from having a good time?

The Army Cadet Force

The ACF gives the following information to those thinking about joining:

> Why join? Because you're 13 to 18 years old. You've got attitude and you want in. To be part of one of the top organizations for young people in the UK. To join over 50,000 members, including 10,000 girls and 8,000 volunteer leaders. All with the same sense of adventure. All who'd do anything for you. There are more than 1,700 Cadet Detachments/Units right across the country. From big cities to small villages, they're everywhere. They're a lot like youth clubs.
>
> It's a youth programme sponsored by the Army and the Ministry of Defence. It's a big opportunity. Seize it and you'll have great fun challenging yourself mentally and physically.

Sea Cadets

The Sea Cadets are a uniformed youth movement with the aim of helping young people towards responsible adulthood by encouraging valuable personal attributes and high standards of conduct using a nautical theme based on Naval customs.

NEED TO KNOW: Time for a mental gear change?

Does your church have a uniformed group attached to it in some way? The most significant single step a church can take in developing the potential of uniformed youth work is to begin recognizing that such groups are already a part of the church's youth work. Too many churches see their Scouts, Guides or Girls' Brigade as a source of income because they rent the hall, or even as competition, taking away valuable leaders and young people. If we begin to see uniformed groups as a part of the Church's youth ministry, we shall stop just asking 'What can they do for us?' and start looking at trying to serve them instead. So what would this mental shift look like if it were to happen?

Belonging

For both the Boys' and Girls' Brigades and the Church Lads' and Church Girls' Brigade, being sponsored by a church is necessary for them to exist. Many active church members see heading up groups in Guiding and Scouting as part of their ministry. However, a surprising number of churches have a youth or youth and children's committee of some sort that has no representation from the uniformed groups at all. The uniformed groups and the 'church's youth work' are in entirely different orbits, even though many of the young people belong to both. If we want uniformed groups and their members to feel like part

> 'If we want uniformed groups and their members to feel like part of the church we need to start including them in our teams and thinking.'

of the church we need to start including them in our teams and thinking. Something as simple as checking a list of dates with each other can prevent a lot of misunderstanding and frustration.

Time

Church leaders need to make time to visit groups to show they care. Many groups, particularly in the younger age range, meet over that difficult teatime when many ministers try to protect their family time. If we want groups to feel included it simply won't do to say, as some church leaders do, that the group meets at a difficult time so I never visit. An occasional look in shows real concern and does make a difference.

Money

What would happen if instead of a group being seen as a source of income for the church it was seen as a ministry of the church? Might a church then provide a budget for its uniformed groups, perhaps so that leaders could attend training or buy new resource books? The subscriptions paid by the young people could then be put into the cost of running the programme rather than paying the rent. More resources are then released and a wider range of activities can be undertaken. If a church shows its priorities through its budget, then we can show a change in thinking by supporting uniformed groups in the same way as other youth work.

Many leaders of uniformed groups feel like forgotten 'bolt-on extras' to the church's work. Most would jump at the chance to build links with the wider Church if they only thought the church was interested in what they do. Youth work is hard work and it is no easier for uniformed leaders. They too struggle to balance work commitments with their leadership, have to deal with young people who let them down and are faced with all the things life throws their way. Many uniformed leaders do feel isolated from the Church and misunderstood. Knowing they are cared for and appreciated would make a world of difference.

CASE STUDY: Making the most of church parade

At least once in a while most uniformed groups end up at church parade. It might be for the Scouting/Guiding 'Thinking Day', or a regular monthly Brigade parade service, or the anniversary of a particular event that brings in the Army Cadets. These opportunities can either be a great advertisement for the church or the final confirmation to the young people that Christianity is boring and irrelevant! So what are parades for and how can we get closer to making them work?

Parades for the openly Christian-based uniformed organizations and for others who are church based can be a bridge to the wider church. They are an opportunity for young people to experience the worship of the church and for the church to recognize the good work of the youth organizations. In this sense they should be a win-win experience for the group and the church. Unfortunately this is often far from the case.

> **'Parades for the openly Christian-based uniformed organizations and for others who are church based can be a bridge to the wider church. They are an opportunity for young people to experience the worship of the church and for the church to recognize the good work of the youth organizations.'**

Most uniformed groups will have more young children than teenagers present at a parade service (apart from the groups connected to the armed services, which recruit only older ages). Puppets and action songs that go down a storm with Cubs and Rainbows are normally totally mortifying to teenagers, who think the idea of singing in public is like having a filling at the dentist (without anaesthetic!). Cross that age line and a fun hour on a Sunday morning becomes humiliation and church becomes a place never to be visited again!

Involvement is key, but it does not always have to be public. Perhaps a church leader could choose the songs together with the young people, or work on prayers or another aspect of the worship with them. Where there are groups with bands they could also play at least some of the songs in the service. Even a very simple thing like making the time to speak to the Flag Party before the service so that they know exactly what to do makes a huge difference.

Swearing in and welcoming new staff at parade services offers an opportunity to pray for leaders and to thank them for the work they put in.

It can also be appropriate to give out awards at parades, making an effort to encourage parents to come and see awards presented. All these are ways of making links and ensuring that the uniformed group is more than an audience watching what is going on.

The final key danger area is the sermon!

Speaking to young people is tough. Speaking to them in the context of an all-age setting is even tougher! However, at least for me, at a parade service the teenagers and young adults should be the target of the talk. Those a little younger will like the idea they are not being spoken to as children, and the very youngest will have other elements in the service that speak to them. Those who are older will, in the main, be able to apply what is being taught to their own situation and probably receive teaching directed at them for the other three Sundays of the month. The opportunity to speak to young people about the Christian faith in the context of worship is simply gold dust. We dare not blow such fantastic opportunities by using boring or irrelevant speakers. It is crucial to find those who can communicate with young people at a parade service. If the church leaders cannot do it themselves then seek out good speakers and book them early!

Are parades the best option for teenagers?

Another option worth thinking about is actively making parade a children's service and providing an alternative for young people, rather than trying to please everyone within a single service. What if older members were sometimes encouraged to attend a local youth event, evening celebration or Christian outreach activity as their 'parade' rather than going to Sunday morning church parade? Might these options be more effective in encouraging young people to think through the faith for themselves than singing 'He's got the whole world in his hands' with six-year-olds?

> 'What if older members were sometimes encouraged to attend a local youth event, evening celebration or Christian outreach activity as their "parade" rather than going to Sunday morning church parade?'

If we want young people in uniformed groups to come to a living faith it is not enough to hope that a parade service or youth event, however creative and impressive, will do the trick. There are many ways the church can increase its support and contact.

Using church members' gifts and skills

The Church Lads' and Girls' Brigade has said that one of its methods is to allow 'children to explore and respond to the Christian Faith as a part of God's family, the Church'. So how can young people meet the church? One key way is by using the gifts and skills found in congregation members. In practice this could mean those who can cook coming in and sharing skills, or those with interesting personal stories that fit in with the programme being interviewed. Imagine the potential if a group is looking at being part of a worldwide organization, and you have a retired missionary in the church with whom they could video an interview! Other people could be brought in to mark badge work; or for an act of service or a hospitality badge, older church folk could be entertained. For this to work leaders need to know what skills are sitting in the congregation, so that church leaders can pro-actively link people and encourage them to work together.

Camps and trips

Extra leaders are almost always needed for annual camps or for trips out. These can be opportunities to mix with other people from church. Residential time away with young people also provides opportunities to create worship experiences completely focused on the age group present. Resources like Youth For Christ's 'Labyrinth' could be ideal in this setting. Youth workers or church leaders are often asked to go as chaplains and this provides a great opportunity. There is a wealth of creative material out there for use by leaders. If you don't know what is available try contacting someone like your Diocesan Youth Officer, if you have one, as they will be a good source of ideas.

Prayer

At the end of the day the effectiveness of a group is not based on the hours and sweat of the leaders or the gifts the young people bring to a group. Making a long-term difference to the lives of the young people is God's work. Many older Christians would love to be informed and pray if only they were given the opportunity.

Integration into the wider church

At some point most young people grow up and leave the uniformed group. Some stay on as leaders but many move away or simply get to the top age and finish their time as a member. How easy do we make it for young people to move from the uniformed group into the church? All too often the honest answer is not very. So what could we do?

- First, we could look for opportunities to do things together with other youth groups in the Church. The 24 Hour Famine organized by World Vision is one ideal opportunity. Joint groups going to events or concerts is another. If we want young people to stay within the church community as they grow out of the uniformed group we must help them build relationships with the wider community.

- Secondly, diocesan and wider events can be used to build links. Too often uniformed groups don't even get the information about leader training or events for young people organized by the wider church. While each uniformed organization provides its own structure of support and training, there could be a massive benefit if the skills of the uniformed groups were shared more widely in a two-way process.

- Finally, what if we saw traditional Bible classes as cell church? Some (uniformed) groups still have a regular Bible class for members. These groups provide teaching and fellowship and in many ways look like an adult-led youth cell group by another name. If those with Bible classes think of them as cell church and tie the cell into that model of church, another way of integration begins to open up.

ALL DRESSED UP

So is developing our work with uniformed groups really worth all the labour? Ask a uniformed group leader or a young person who came to faith through such a group and the answer will of course be yes. There is another reason why doing good uniformed work is so important. Most of those who have been through a uniformed group keep a special place in their hearts for them. 'Once a Scout always a Scout' many not be universally true but there is something which does stay with many people. In market towns and areas where people tend not to move on, this means uniformed groups can have a generational impact that really lasts.

Despite difficulties in holding on to teenagers, uniformed youth work still provides a great opportunity for the Church. The numbers of ministers and leaders in the Church today who came to faith through these groups are testimony to their positive impact. With a new sense of support and cooperation between the church and uniformed group leaders there is no reason why together we should not go on bringing many young people into all that God intends for their lives.

ALL DRESSED UP

More details about uniformed groups can be found on their web sites. Many also include useful resources and ideas as well as lists of local group meetings.

Boys' Brigade: www.boys-brigade.org.uk
Girls' Brigade: www.girlsbrigadeew.org.uk
Church Lads' and Church Girls' Brigade: www.clcgb.org.uk
Scouting UK: www.scouts.org.uk
Girlguiding UK: www.girlguiding.org.uk

Air Cadets: www.aircadets.org
Army Cadets: www.armycadets.com
Sea Cadets: www.sea-cadets.org

World Vision's 24 Hour Famine can be found at
www.24hourfamine.org.uk

The Labyrinth kit for a guided journey of prayer and meditation for young people is available from Youth for Christ www.yfc.co.uk

4 STARTING FROM SCRATCH: Reaching young people when you don't have any

Matt Elsey

INTRODUCTION: Help – where do I start?

Believing in work with young people is one thing. Establishing work with young people when your church doesn't have any to start with is an entirely different problem. This chapter tells the story of how I tried to develop youth work without a building, a team, or any young people from the local area. That is the situation I found myself facing when I was appointed as a youth and community worker in South Wigston, Leicestershire. This is a warts and all chapter where I share not only the successes but also the deep frustrations of trying to build work with young people from scratch. I hope that both the good and the frustrating insights and experiences will encourage anyone thinking about establishing a new youth ministry project, whether they are employed by the church or are a volunteer.

THE ISSUE: Starting from nowhere

The issue is easy enough to define: more than 50 per cent of churches in the UK have no young people regularly attending (although Church of England statistics show a slight increase over the last few years).[1] We can get really excited about equipping young people to share their faith, or helping them engage in their local communities, but unless we have a group of young people to work with all we have is a mixture of hope and frustration. So how can we turn a desire to work with young people into a reality?

> 'How can we turn a desire to work with young people into a reality?'

Let me tell you how I came face to face with the reality behind this frightening problem. The Leicester Castle Salvation Army had been based in the centre of the city of Leicester for over 100 years. Because of a range of factors it was decided to relocate the church to another area of Leicester. It is now based in a small town south of the city. The Salvation Army had not been actively working in this area before and it was felt that it would be useful to have a full-time worker in the local community before the church as a whole moved into the area. I was appointed in November 2002 with no knowledge of the locality or when the new church building would be built.

In terms of our church's youth provision, we had little apart from a Youth Fellowship (Sunday night) and cell group (Wednesday). We are blessed with a number of young adults in our church, but only one or two 12–18-year-olds. We found ourselves faced with the challenge of turning our desire to work with local young people into a living reality as·we began building youth work in this new place from scratch.

BACKGROUND: Starting out

One of the steepest learning curves I had to face was how to integrate myself into a community and become familiar and recognized within it! Living in the area is a good place to start but not always essential in the short term. One of the ways that I found helpful was to begin by going out rather than trying to get young people to come to me. I joined in with existing groups within the area such as a toy library, Development Workers' Forum, youth club, detached youth work with the County Council, Churches Together, and the local Voluntary Sector Forum. This way I got a real feel for what was going on, an idea of the local cultures and also of the types of young people I might be working with in the future. It also sent a message to the wider community that I was there not just for the church, but for everyone.

> 'One of the steepest learning curves I had to face was how to integrate myself into a community and become familiar and recognized within it!'

From my experience over the last three years, I believe there are two key factors that support the development of new mission to young people. They are Community and Commitment. Without these two components no work with young people can grow and develop. With them it is possible to see work grow, although it will remain costly – there is no quick fix in developing work with young people.

Community

The term 'community' is a minefield! It has so many connotations. So first of all it is key that you determine what you mean by 'community' in your setting. It could be a geographical area or different group(s) of young people. Always be mindful of the physical area you are working in as well; this will allow you to know where people are talking about in meetings and conversation and help you fit in.

The key to any kind of existing or new community is how relationships are built and maintained, Community within a group of young people is built through who you are and how you communicate your faith through your life. Building community with young people takes time and is hugely frustrating for long periods but also a privilege and a tool for growth in your own spiritual journey. Time is an important factor in this process. Giving the time to listen to young people is important. Often our youth programmes are so full of activities that keep young people busy we never have a chance to get to know them! Starting from scratch allows for relationships to take priority over programme. Then in time we can build programmes and activities together with those young people with whom we have built new relationships. Working with them will increase the sense of community because it shows that we take their input seriously.

> **'Giving the time to listen to young people is important. Often our youth programmes are so full of activities that keep young people busy we never have a chance to get to know them! Starting from scratch allows for relationships to take priority over programme.'**

One of the hardest but most important things to do is to justify to the supporting church the way in which you spend your time and why, particularly if they are expecting to see young people start attending regular church services as a result of your ministry. It is a natural instinct for them and you to want to see results but this will not happen overnight. That means helping the wider church to understand that what you are doing is really important so that they have realistic expectations.

Commitment

It might sound obvious, but there are some realities in being committed to ministry that are often overlooked, especially when it comes to working with young people. There are some costs to be worked through as you build community and relationships.

On first arrival you will have worked out where the young people are, and having been in the community for a while you will have to start making decisions about what you do and don't do. This could be in terms of outreach, volunteering, time off and also beginning to develop your own limited programme. You need to balance where the need is and also what local young people are into. Where the gaps are and how to fill them is where you should start. To begin with it is all about creating contact points. We used a football weekend at the end of the season; we also ran a number of craft events at specific times of the year, for example Christmas, Easter and Harvest; and we had a summer playscheme for younger children. All these activities have created a list of contacts with both the young people and their parents. We can now move forward and start to look at regular and more evangelistic

'To begin with it is all about creating contact points. We used a football weekend at the end of the season; we also ran a number of craft events at specific times of the year, for example Christmas, Easter and Harvest; and we had a summer playscheme for younger children. All these activities have created a list of contacts with both the young people and their parents.'

opportunities. Too much programme too soon could actually have a negative impact on your ability to build relationships at this foundational stage for your ministry, because you won't have time to get to know and understand the young people. These are all practical things that you must deal with. You must also put your personal 'spiritual life' at the top of the priorities for you and your work. If your spiritual wellbeing takes a pounding so will your effectiveness and enthusiasm for God. That has a knock-on effect with those around you. To think that you are the only one doing anything of worth is foolish. There are often other people around just waiting to be asked to help, so ask them!

When there are no young people a lot of commitment will be expected of you as the person with responsibility for finding some! Commitment to a vision, role or mission is vital but make sure you are clear on your parameters of time, accountability, the expectations of others and relationships with family and friends.

NEED TO KNOW: Starting from scratch can hurt

Starting a new work with young people raises many practical issues and emotions for the individual(s) pioneering the effort. Here are some of the concerns and areas I discovered that I needed to face. They are not unique to my situation but are likely to be faced by anyone in a similar position.

Loneliness

Establishing new work can get very lonely at times, so look for the signs early. Building relationships with young people can be frustrating and if you are a lone worker it can feel like 'me against the world'. Loneliness is dangerous because it can lead to a sense of failure or an over-analysis of your work. Keep yourself aware of all the good work that is going on around you in both a Christian and a secular context. It was also important for me

> 'Loneliness is dangerous because it can lead to a sense of failure or an over-analysis of your work. Keep yourself aware of all the good work that is going on around you in both a Christian and a secular context.'

to meet with Christian and non-Christian workers for coffee and to talk about what was happening in the community. Partnership work is not only a good use of resources but also a great tool for being encouraged and for building relationships. Seeing yourself as one link in a chain will help combat that sense of loneliness. Try to rejoice in the small steps you are making and in the connections and relationships with other workers. This attitude will both encourage you and focus your mind on what you are doing rather than what you haven't yet done!

One of the key things in any ministry is being able to talk through issues and situations with others. You need to find someone you can trust and with whom you can share anything and everything. They need to be able to listen and help you work through the issues at hand. It will also encourage you that you don't have to deal with the issues alone, knowing that you have prayer and practical support from someone.

Time management

One of the the hardest things about ministry is how you manage your time, particularly if you have a job and work with young people as a volunteer. There will be so many people, situations, clubs, personal circumstances that want your attention and time! Remember that you are no good to God if you are being burnt out in your ministry – but it still happens far too often. Be on guard that you are not so busy that you forget why you do what you do. Always make time for God and for your family and friends. Your work is important but so is your own state of spirit and your key relationships! Anyone in ministry always feels guilty about not doing something or guilty about taking time off. Don't be tempted to overwork to get things off the ground; you won't be able to keep it up!

> 'Anyone in ministry always feels guilty about not doing something or guilty about taking time off. Don't be tempted to overwork to get things off the ground; you won't be able to keep it up!'

Frustration

Frustration in ministry is a double-edged sword. Frustration is a pain in the neck and the biggest danger that leads people to give up ministry or to feel a failure. On the other side, frustration keeps us on our toes, moving us forwards to impact the young people with whom we come into contact. I was once told that you could not have vision without a sense of frustration and dissatisfaction with the present. With young people you are always going to see potential but they will also disappoint you week in and week out because they are still learning; they often just forget to turn up, or maybe don't fully understand what you do or why you do it! When you begin with no young people this effect is multiplied. A youth group of 30 may not notice if 5 of its number are at a school concert but when you only have 5 young people anyway it is disastrous! It can be really disappointing to spend time building relationships in the hope that young people will come to Christ and yet see little visible result. God is powerful and a miracle worker but only when the time is right. Remember it's his will not ours, we are simply the messenger – so don't try and rush on faster than God is going! Try to avoid comparing your results with others. Keeping in mind we are not in competition with other churches and youth workers is an important discipline.

Communication

Communication is often assumed rather than worked on. Don't expect every member in your church to ask what you do or how it is going. Do not assume that they will try and find out from you, or read the minutes of meetings. Be as transparent as possible in what you do and about the situations you find yourself in: the troubles, the frustrations, the joys and progress. People are slow at asking but once they know and understand what you are doing and why, they will support you with time, prayer and resources.

It is also well worth making clear to the young people you are trying to work with who you are and why you do what you do. Communicate with the young people's schools, families, colleges and social circles. Young people always want you to be upfront; they respect that and will respond to it over time. Be honest in your communication and don't try and hide things from the young people; they will soon find you out! The bottom line is that community is about the relationships that you build and the effort you put into them. It is that which allows you to become credible within a community. Being genuine is key!

CASE STUDY: Running before I could walk

I have been volunteering for three years at a local youth club run by a parent from South Wigston. We met at an event and she invited me to come and help. Through the club I have been able to connect with over 70 young people. I just hang around, chat, play pool and show a loving interest in the young people's lives. When you have no young people you need to go to where they are. You will probably find so much going on in your community already: get involved and you will often have the opportunity to speak for Christ into young people's lives. However, it took about a year for me to be accepted as part of the group. We have seen some of these young people link up with events and activities that we have held, such as our football weekends and craft days, and we even had one lad on work experience for a week.

When I had been in the community for about seven months I decided to hold a mission week in the May half term. As part of the week I held a free car wash in a local car park. I washed one car and two bikes in two hours. I thought that this time would allow me to really connect with the community but instead I felt I had failed and was totally deflated. If I then told you that I did this on my own you would then start to see why it didn't work. Mission is about relationship! The car wash had no relevance because of the lack of relationships. If I said to my neighbour, 'Can I wash you car?' they would let me because they know and trust me more than some strangers in a car park. This principle highlights the pitfall of thinking you are busy doing a good thing when really you have missed the point altogether. I know I did, and have learnt from it.

THINKING IT THROUGH

How do you guard against being lonely?

- Can you link with others who share a vision for reaching young people in your area? Can you find other interests to meet people and help you switch off?
- Try to see God's view: that you are one link in a very big chain!
- Are you praying?
- Allow God to speak to you as well as you speaking to God, and ask others to pray for your ministry and needs. Make and share a list of prayers that have been answered and say 'Thank You'!

Time management

- How many hours do you work (including all the extra bits!)?
- Do you spend enough time with family and friends?
- Make sure you say 'no' when your diary is nearly full, not when you are already double booked!
- Can you find someone who will honestly tell you to do less/more in ministry when needed?

What existing networks are in place to work with?

- Schools might be a good start. Discover where they are and the age ranges they serve. Could you offer to be involved in some way? Ask how you could support them, not just what opportunities they could offer you.
- Are there are any local sports clubs where you could offer to help, for example with coaching?

Frustrations and encouragements

- Are you willing to get frustrated and keep going?
- Are you willing to give God the glory for what you achieve?
- Who can you share your frustration with?
- Remember what encourages you inside and outside the church.

STARTING FROM SCRATCH

Beginning new work with young people means balancing many wants, people, needs and expectations as you travel on your journey. It will be lonely, it will be frustrating but the glory that you bring to God through hard work, determination and keeping going will be received with thanks and a resounding AMEN from the Angels in Heaven. Take encouragement from Paul's words in Philippians 4.8-9 (*New Living Bible*):

> And now, dear brothers and sisters, let me say one more thing as I close this letter. Fix your thoughts on what is true and honourable and right. Think about things that are pure and lovely and admirable. Think about things that are excellent and worthy of praise. Keep putting into practice all you learned from me and saw me doing, and the God of peace will be with you. Amen.

Keep going and be amazed by God!

STARTING FROM SCRATCH

The following web sites all have ideas and stories to encourage and support those setting out on the adventure of establishing new work.

www.youthworker.co.uk
www.freshexpressions.org.uk
www.emergingchurch.info
www.salvationarmy.org.uk/alove

5 TAKING A GAP YEAR: How to tell a great opportunity from a costly mistake

David Booker

INTRODUCTION: So many choices

Every year hundreds of young people take the opportunity to engage in mission through a gap year with Christian organizations and churches in the UK and abroad. Some schemes really do live up to their advertisements, offering fantastic opportunities to pick up new skills and grow in faith. Unfortunately, others can leave their volunteers disappointed and disillusioned with the Church and their faith. This chapter aims to help clergy and youth leaders support young people in making wise decisions about where to invest their year and to consider how to support them once the year ends.

THE ISSUE: The good, the bad and the ugly gap years

Sara took a year out working at the church she joined while attending university. It was a great year for her faith and personal development. She learnt new skills and grew in confidence as she was given responsibility for leading small groups and occasionally speaking at youth events. She and the other gap year team members attended staff team meetings and were given regular support and teaching from the senior staff. However, at the end of her year she lost that special relationship with the leadership team and new gap year workers took over her roles with the young people. While at one level she knew she had been in a privileged position that could not last, the loss of status and time with the church leaders left her feeling abandoned, rejected and useless as she watched others receiving the time and encouragement that had made her feel so special. After six months of trying to find a new role for herself she drifted away entirely, full of bitterness towards the Church.

Mark joined the same gap year team as Sara. He was asked to work part time with the church's youth worker at the end of his year, particularly developing the work in local schools. A year later Mark replaced the youth worker when he moved on to a new post. Mark is now an effective, gifted and passionate full-time youth worker.

Having worked nationally for Church Army, and as a Diocesan Youth Officer, I met many young people like Mark. They were always a real encouragement to me, a sign that positive outcomes are often the result of a gap year. Unfortunately I have also met too many Saras in my time. Good, committed, willing people who have been hurt and relegated to the sidelines or who have even left the Church altogether because of what they experienced in their year out or at the end of it.

However, don't be put off just because an individual's year can occasionally go wrong. The potential for young people to discover their gifts and vocations during gap years is immense and most of them have a great time! It can lead them in all sorts of exciting directions, not necessarily paid ministry, but into jobs and roles they may never have considered before. A well-supported year can be a real investment in the future. So what can leaders do to ensure the Church sees fewer casualties and more successes though gap year opportunities?

> 'The potential for young people to discover their gifts and vocations during gap years is immense and most of them have a great time! It can lead them in all sorts of exciting directions, not just paid ministry, but into jobs and roles they may never have considered before. A well-supported year can be a real investment in the future.'

THEORY: Why and where?

There are plenty of good reasons for a young Christian to consider taking a gap year before beginning work or university. Some people take a year out to test a vocation towards a form of full-time ministry or as a way of taking stock and thinking about which way they should go next in life. For others it might be a year to develop new skills and talents together with experience to put onto a CV. Others choose a gap year so they can grow in their faith and deepen their understanding of who God is. Some see the year as their chance to be involved in an inspiring project or to work with a person they admire; for others it is a chance to 'put something back' by serving the church or community. All of these are good reasons. In reality most young people exploring a gap year will come with a whole mix of these feelings and desires motivating them.

The reasons behind gap year providers offering the opportunity of a year working with their particular organization or project are of course just as varied. Inevitably for most the primary reason they advertise is that they want to maintain and develop their work. However caring and supportive providers are, young people need help to remember that the first reason there may be a place for them is so that they can work for the organization they sign up with. Any training offered, however good it may be, is going to be secondary to the task they are asked to fulfil. If a young person primarily wants training for the future they should probably be looking at colleges rather than gap years as their first choice. This means that beneath the glossy promotional material and the kudos of working with a particular organization, prospective volunteers need to ask themselves if they really want to spend a year doing the particular task they will be asked to do. I once met a group of thoroughly disillusioned UK gap year volunteers when speaking at a youth conference overseas. The glitz of being based abroad and of working with a 'big name' leader had soon worn off when they became bored with the mundane day-to-day tasks they were given. A good rule of thumb seems to be 'If you wouldn't be happy to do the job here then you won't be happy doing the same job in Africa!'

Alongside the desire for workers, gap year providers can have a variety of other motivations, both explicitly acknowledged and more hidden. For some there is a hope that volunteers will go on to become full-time workers. For others the fees young people pay support the ongoing ministry of the project as well as meeting the young person's expenses. Other groups hope the experience of the year will lead volunteers to become lifelong supporters of their cause or project.

Given the wide variety of providers, it is possible to find a year out doing just about anything. Whether it's digging wells, teaching English, working in schools and with young people, supporting an outward bound centre and gaining qualifications as an instructor, or making beds in a retreat house, the option will be out there somewhere.

NEED TO KNOW: It's a volunteers' market!

There are somewhere around 150 Christian organizations offering year out opportunities in the UK alone. Most of those have more potential spaces each year than volunteers to fill them. That means young people can and should be choosy in their selection. However, young people can too often end up feeling that organizations are doing them a great favour in letting them volunteer for a year. This may be a useful understanding for organizations to promote, but it does nothing to help young people develop the ability to carefully discern their way forward. Knowing organizations are often crying out for volunteers should give young people the time and the space to really think through what they want to do and who they want to work with. Having said that, it is of course crucial that young people are willing to be servants of whichever project they finally sign up with. Choosing a gap year is not the same a picking out a package holiday, where the main demand is self-comfort and enjoyment.

> 'It is of course crucial that young people are willing to be servants of whichever project they finally sign up with. Choosing a gap year is not the same a picking out a package holiday, where the main demand is self-comfort and enjoyment.'

Inevitably, every scheme will also have its share of disappointing outcomes where for a variety of personal, practical or cultural reasons young people don't complete their year out. Working with young people is always a risk and some young people will not see it through because their circumstances change or for other good reasons. No matter how foolproof a selection is, or how committed a young person is, no scheme will be perfect and not every volunteer will see through their year. However, some schemes and projects seem to have more than their fair share of horror stories. Here are some key issues to bear in mind when helping a young person consider the options available to them.

How easy is it to get a place?

How much does an organization want to know about its potential workers? Do they take up references? Do they interview in person? The more effort organizations put into discovering how the people who apply are motivated and what skills they bring the better they will be able to place them. If a gap year provider doesn't want to get to know its perspective volunteers, how can it know who is right for them? Be careful: if it's too easy to join the project it may mean they are desperate to fill up their spaces.

A gap year is not a blind date!

Some schemes sign young people up, take their money, give them two weeks' induction and only then tell them where they are going to be based for the year. This approach demands huge amounts of trust on the part of the young person, who never gets to check the opportunity out in advance. This hardly seems like the way to treat responsible, discerning adults and these high-risk schemes do seem to have higher rates of drop out.

What about the small print?

Some schemes place young people in one 'home' for the whole time they are with them; others move team members about during the year. Thinking about where the young person will be living is a key factor in whether or not a year is survivable. Will it feel like their own space, a place where they can relax, or will it feel as if they are always 'on duty' even when not working? It is also worth checking what stance the organization or church has on romantic relationships between team members or with team members and

> 'Before signing the year away it really is important to check out the rules and expectations. If the young person can live with them, then great, but volunteering for a year of fighting the rules is a recipe for disaster for all concerned.'

others. Some projects ban any romantic attachments while on their scheme. Such a stance may well have good reasons behind it, but can seem both harsh and hard to enforce! Before signing the year away it really is important to check out the rules and expectations. If the young person can live with them, then great, but volunteering for a year of fighting the rules is a recipe for disaster for all concerned.

What if it goes wrong?

Is there a code of behaviour expected of volunteers? Is there a clearly laid-down disciplinary procedure? What happens if things are not working out? These questions can be much harder if working on a project set up by a single local church where there is no national structure or support worker to draw in. On the other hand, working for a local church rather than a national scheme can mean volunteers have a clearer idea at the outset of what is expected of them. National projects should have a worker that volunteers can call on to mediate, and if it all goes wrong, they can often have the option of moving to another project.

Money!

While there are still some 'free' gap year opportunities, most make some charge towards the cost of the year. The figures can range from a few hundred pounds to anything up to £3,500. Good providers will not only be clear about the cost, but also explain clearly how the money given is spent and provide ideas for young people looking to fund their year. Inevitably, high fees put many young people off some opportunities, particularly with the growth of student debt also a worry. Overseas gap years are particularly costly.

Different schemes use the payment they receive in different ways. Young people need to be sure they know what is covered and what is not and also need to allow for 'pocket money' for themselves because increasingly this is not paid by gap year providers. Understanding the payment of expenses is another key area with which young people are likely to be unfamiliar. The young person applying should treat any scheme that doesn't meet out-of-pocket expenses with real care; this is very poor practice but still happens fairly regularly. If young people do not know the cost involved, or how they are going to raise it, alarm bells should be ringing loudly.

Walk, don't run!

One of the biggest problems for young people selecting their year out option is simply leaving it too late. Looking for a gap year in July to start that September is bound to be more rushed and less considered than looking early at the options. The rule here is simple – the earlier the search starts the less likely a mistake will be made!

CASE STUDY: It can work!

Martin was thinking of taking a year out. At a major conference he was given a handful of glossy leaflets from the smiling reps of a range of organizations. Each had a fairly similar process for selecting young people, each promised a year that would change his life and would deepen his faith. As he read them he soon realized there were also more than a few differences. While some were free others wanted up to £3,500 for the privilege of working with them. That kind of figure was way beyond his small church and modestly earning parents, so they were rejected early on. Finally he made a choice of two organizations and applied to both. On the basis of the interviews he had, both schemes offered him a place working in large churches as assistant to the employed youth worker. One scheme offered him two residential training events during the year and visits from a regional support worker alongside the support from the local church. That extra support ultimately swayed his choice and he signed up for the year.

There was the inevitable blur of new names and faces when he began, but slowly they began to make sense and he found his feet. He found the change in the way people saw him quite surprising. In a weekend he had moved from a member of a youth group to being seen as a leader who was asked questions and whose behaviour was watched and commented upon by the young people. He often felt unworthy and inexperienced but with the support of the youth worker and wider church he found his feet. Martin developed leadership and pastoral skills in the cell group he led and was able to talk about his newly found confidence when applying to university. He did have times of frustration and at least once was ready to pick up the phone and pack it all in, but he managed to stick it out even through the disappointments. When he went back home people told him how much he had grown, which both pleased and rather surprised him.

Martin now teaches in a secondary school. As he looks back he sees that his gap year was a real turning point in deciding which way to go. Through the work he did Martin discovered his ability and enjoyment of teaching and he has never looked back. Not every gap year goes like Martin's, but when young people think carefully about their options rather than rushing at the first advert they see, very many do.

> **'Martin now teaches in a secondary school. As he looks back he sees that his gap year was a real turning point in deciding which way to go.'**

THINKING IT THROUGH

Here are some of the key questions to help church leaders in their support of young people considering taking a gap year. The first section is for the church leader and explores the church's role in support; the second section has questions the leader should help young people work through in the process of choosing their option.

Questions for the leader/supporting church

- How can the sending church organize prayer, practical and financial support?
- How can the church be kept in touch with the young person's work during the year?
- How can the sending church's leader or youth leader support the volunteer while they are away, or is it going to be a case of out of sight and out of mind?
- Who will help the young person adapt to 'ordinary' church life once they have finished their year, or will they just be left to find their own way?
- Does the group they spend the year with feel a sense of obligation to its volunteers after the year is over?
- How can you help young people to reflect on their 'gap year experience'?

Questions young people should work through

- What do you want to get out of the year/achieve through doing it? Is your intention really to serve or simply to put off university or work for a year of having fun?
- How does taking a year out fit into your ongoing plan for your future life?
- How are you going to stay in touch with your sending church?
- Is a gap year the best choice or could you get similar experience working for a year? Even if a year out is right, is it therefore right to spend it with a Christian organization or would you grow and be more challenged with another year out provider?
- How much can you afford or can you raise towards your year out?
- Have you worked out what the cost of the year really might be and drawn up a budget? Don't forget to include items like mobile phone, travelling home and back for holidays and pocket money to go for a coffee or see a film. Even simple things like buying toothpaste will need to be paid for from somewhere!!

TAKING A GAP YEAR

SUMMARY

Gap years can be life changing, faith enhancing, amazing adventures. As a way of gaining practical experience, serving God and testing out skills they are hard to beat. By asking the right questions and being wise in their selection of gap year provider, young people can avoid many of the potential pitfalls and disappointments some people experience. All ministry involves a level of risk and no choice is ever foolproof. However, wise support and appropriate critical analysis of the options and the young person's motivations by supportive leaders can help young people avoid costly mistakes.

TAKING A GAP YEAR

All the major mission agencies carry details of their schemes on their web sites and many large churches run their own schemes. A search on the web will reveal many of these options.

The greatest single evangelical resource on gap years is the annually produced *Short Term Service Directory* from Christian Vocations. It has details of over 100 different schemes together with helpful information and advice. www.christianvocations.org

BEYOND THE CHURCH WALLS

Mission by its very nature forces us to look beyond where we already are. As we follow God's lead we will find ourselves taken outside areas where we feel comfortable to the broken places where God intends the healing of his kingdom to be made manifest. The chapters in this second section are intended to raise our vision beyond what we can achieve now to where we should be heading in the future if we want to see our mission with and to young people develop.

Firstly we explore two ways of working with young people where they are. Debbie Orriss, who has been both a classroom teacher and a schools worker employed by the church, explores some of the rationale behind schools work and shares some of the opportunities for Christians to work in partnership with their local schools. Diana Greenfield then shares some ways of serving and witnessing to clubbers. Diana has a wide experience of the diversity of club life and of developing teams who can work effectively in this challenging environment.

Issues of religious tolerance, or the lack of it, are regularly in the news. However, rather than loving, serving and witnessing, we often ignore those from other faith communities. Deep down we know the good news is for all people, not simply those like us, but it can be hard to know where to start in responding to those with other faiths. In my chapter 'Ignorance is bliss?' I explore how we can equip our young people to live faithful to Christ in a world where many faiths live alongside each other.

Poverty and environmental change are real concerns to many young people. Both of these issues are represented in the Five Marks of Mission through its calls

> to respond to human needs by loving service;
> to seek to transform unjust structures of society;
> to strive to safeguard the integrity of creation, to sustain and renew the life of the earth.

Martin Parks, a Christian Aid youth coordinator, looks at why poverty matters and how we can help young people both to understand it and to take action. Martyn Lings, who works for A Rocha, a Christian environmental charity, then looks at our responsibility to equip young people to care for the world God created. Both these chapters again challenge any narrow definition of mission and show how God's people are called to work for the good of God's world in many situations.

6 CLASS ACT: Developing work with schools

Debbie Orriss

INTRODUCTION: Opportunity knocks

'Does God know whether Man Utd are going to beat Juventus?' This question was asked by an 11-year-old boy who attended a lunchtime club I ran in a comprehensive school. Although this was, in part, an attempt to give his mates a laugh, there was also, I believe, a pertinent 'question behind the question': 'Does God really know everything? Does he know me?' What followed was a really interesting discussion with the group about whether God was restricted by time or outside of it. To me, the question is an example of the many opportunities that exist for young people to explore faith, through appropriate Christian ministry in schools.

THE ISSUE: Find young people . . . in a school near you

You would probably not be surprised to know that recent statistics have shown that church attendance has reduced dramatically over the last 30 years, particularly among those under the age of 20 (although Church of England statistics show a slight increase over the last few years).[1] Churches are recognizing these trends and are aware that it is not appropriate in our increasingly post-Christian society to wait for young people to walk through the church doors. We need to go to where they are, and most young people spend a great deal of their waking hours in school.

When you hear the word 'school' a range of thoughts and images may come into your mind – some negative, and hopefully, some positive! The experience of school is hugely influential for young people as they explore relationships, the world and their place within it. Emlyn Williams develops this point and provides three very good reasons for getting involved in schools in his book *The Schools Work Handbook*:[2]

> Schools are a crucial part of any wider community: 'Some have likened the school gate to the biblical well – the hub of a community. Over the past few years schools have developed closer links with the wider community, open to involvement and support from "outside".'

Schools are not 'neutral' – the values, whether they be implicit or explicit, will affect the young person, and have a major impact on the kind of adults they become.

Schools offer opportunity for individuals to grow; 'From a Christian point of view we rejoice when people are given a different and better future . . . the gospel is at the heart of the better future that God desires for each of His children.'

THEORY: Schools need us

As Christians we can often be involved in helping young people in their exploration of the world through supporting schools; what's more, current legislation encourages schools to ask Christians to be involved in the curriculum. Sometimes we are tempted to believe that only church schools offer us opportunity, but according to the 1988 Education Reform Act the school curriculum should promote:

> The spiritual, moral, cultural, mental, and physical development of pupils at the school and of society.[3]

While religious education:

> should seek: to develop pupils' knowledge, understanding and awareness of Christianity, as the predominant religion in Great Britain, and other principal religions represented in the country; to encourage respect for those holding different beliefs; and to help promote pupils' spiritual, moral, cultural and mental development.[4]

'As Christians we can often be involved in helping young people in their exploration of the world through supporting schools; what's more, current legislation encourages schools to ask Christians to be involved in the curriculum.'

Concerning collective worship, all schools must provide a daily act of collective worship and the

> majority of acts of worship over a term must be wholly or mainly of a broadly Christian character.[5]

Another significant development from the 1988 Education Reform Act has been the National Curriculum. Although RE is not part of the National Curriculum, one result of its introduction has been a more systematic treatment of Religious Education, with each education authority developing an Agreed Syllabus for this area of the curriculum. The position of RE was further strengthened by the introduction of a National Framework for RE in 2004.[6]

Consequently, schools have to provide young people with particular opportunities such as visits to places of worship and interviews with people who profess a particular religious belief. These educational developments, and other new developments like the government's support for Extended Schools, have opened up huge opportunities for Christian input.[7]

There are also ways in which Christians can be involved in a more incarnational way, through being 'salt and light' within the school community: supporting young people with special needs, working with a group on the school garden, or being a governor. Christians can also be involved, of course, by supporting and praying for teachers and all those who work in schools. Further suggestions are listed at the end of this chapter.

> 'There are also ways in which Christians can be involved in a more incarnational way, through being 'salt and light' within the school community: supporting young people with special needs, working with a group on the school garden, or being a governor.'

A local response

It's likely that those churches which recognize their inability to make contact with young people through church-based activities are also those that do not have the financial resources to fund a schools worker. However, groups of churches are increasingly joining together to support a worker, or often a team of people, in their local schools. This happened in the Laughton Deanery within the Sheffield Diocese. One of the clergy, the Revd Philip Ireson, had a particular commitment to young people. His vision was for a project, jointly supported by a group of parishes in this semi-rural, ex-mining area of South Yorkshire, which would focus on the schools rather than on church-based activities.

After months of prayer, meetings and consultations, the Laughton Deanery Schools Project was launched in 1995 and I was appointed as full-time Schools Worker in 1997. The Project was funded jointly by the Sheffield Diocese, the Anglican mission agency Church Army, individuals and the nine parishes in the southern half of the deanery, together with some limited secular sources.

The area covered by the Project included 2 comprehensive schools, 13 primary schools and 1 special school, across an area of approximately 20 square miles. I realized very quickly that I would need to be Superwoman to be effective across such a large area! I also firmly believe that ministry in schools is not just the domain of ex-schoolteachers or clergy! Consequently we developed a team of volunteers which included retired people, young people, a young man who worked in the Project as a gap year placement and a local Methodist layworker, who worked part-time for the Project.

The aims of the Schools Project were:

> to give young people access to traditional forms of spirituality;
> to support young people pastorally through its work and to encourage young people to explore the claims of the Christian faith for themselves;
> to support local primary and secondary schools in any ways that the schools required.[8]

This was not a project developed by a big church with lots of money. Plenty of hard work and sweat went into bringing the Project together, but it does show what can be achieved when working across traditional boundaries.

'This was not a project developed by a big church with lots of money. Plenty of hard work and sweat went into bringing the Project together, but it does show what can be achieved when working across traditional boundaries.'

NEED TO KNOW: Open doors

What follows is some of the ways in which Christians can serve their local schools, including some examples from the work of the Schools Project.

Collective worship

Schools are educational establishments and young people have no choice about their attendance. Therefore it is inappropriate to proselytize in collective worship or lessons. However, it is possible to share faith, provided that certain boundaries are kept. The language used in schools is very important. It must be what Emlyn Williams describes as 'non-presumptive':

> If we want people to hear what we say and not what they think we say, we have to pay attention to the words we use. 'Non-presumptive' language recognizes that not everyone will agree with us and that we are ready to justify what we say. When we use it, we are not saying that truth is relative, or that it doesn't matter what you believe.[9]

The following phrases are useful when working in school:

> 'Christians believe . . .'
> 'As a Christian I believe that . . .'
> 'It seems to me . . .'
> 'I think . . .'
> 'The Bible says . . .'
> 'In my experience . . .'
> 'Would you agree that . . .?'

Collective worship and lessons provide significant opportunities to share the Christian faith with both staff and pupils. In comprehensive schools, collective worship tends to focus on encouraging young people to think about issues of faith and keep an open mind. By the time they reach secondary age there is more pressure on young people to dismiss Christianity as being distinctly 'uncool'. Also schools, as we have already considered, are not neutral and can often present a very humanistic view of society and the world, so collective worship may help provide a balanced view. Themes such as 'gossip', 'God of surprises', 'being unique/special', 'respect' and 'peer pressure' are relevant, and are often positively received by both pupils and staff.

> 'Collective worship and lessons provide significant opportunities to share the Christian faith with both staff and pupils.'

In one act of collective worship I talked about how I believed that God isn't interested in what trainers we can afford to wear (having spoken about the poverty I had encountered in Kenya), or how intelligent we are: he simply loves us. A teacher came up to me afterwards and told me that another member of staff had held up a pair of expensive trainers in a previous assembly and told the young people that if they wanted to be able to afford trainers like these, they would have to work hard to get their exams! I wasn't necessarily contradicting what he'd said, but the different use of the illustration obviously spoke powerfully to that member of staff, and hopefully to some of the young people!

On another occasion, after we used a sketch where two people were talking about proving the existence of God, I went on to talk about how we can't put God in a box, there will always be some mystery that we can't explain, but the mystery doesn't disprove God. A teacher followed me out to my car specifically to tell me that I had challenged his view of God.

Such contributions to a school's collective worship aim to present aspects of the Christian faith in an enjoyable way, and hopefully provide a positive view of Christians, the Church and, most importantly, God. The aim is that, as a result, young people are at least more open-minded towards the Christian faith, although they are less likely to be as openly positive towards your input as the school staff, particularly given that their mates will be watching their every move!

Visits to places of worship

Visits to a local church provide great opportunities to tell the Christian story using the building and all the images it contains. Many schools have visits to churches as part of their RE lessons. If this is made into a positive experience young people are far more likely to think positively of any other contact they have with the Church. It is therefore worth putting time and energy into getting it right. David Lankshear's book, *Churches Serving Schools* (see resources list) provides a very helpful checklist for preparing for a school visit, including making use of the buildings, information on the meaning of Christian symbols, and many practical pointers for helping everything run smoothly.

RE lessons

In secondary schools it is appropriate to offer to go in and talk about one's faith from personal experience, but again we must be sensitive to using 'non-presumptive language'. In one school I had some amazing opportunities to share my faith story, but it took several meetings with the head of the RE department to gain those opportunities: several years before, a group of Christians had gone into one of her lessons, given their testimonies and then asked the class to come to the front if they wanted to give their lives to Christ, warning them that they could end up in hell if they did not take this opportunity to respond! Needless to say they were never invited back.

> **'In secondary schools it is appropriate to offer to go in and talk about one's faith from personal experience, but again we must be sensitive to using "non-presumptive language".'**

Supporting other lessons

David Lankshear's *Churches Serving Schools* again includes tips on how churches can form links and support music, history and the arts subjects as well as offering more general support to the school. We have resources to offer that many schools would be only too glad to make use of.

Special services

Many schools still have a carol service and often welcome creative support in putting everything together. Youth leaders and clergy can develop drama or other creative contributions to the service by working together with young people. Hosting school Christingle services and celebrations of the school community in church are a great start. On one occasion, a youngster from one of the primary schools with which I worked came to a church for a service marking the end of the school year. He was not at all happy about coming into the building, so as he approached I greeted him at the door and asked him what was the matter. His reply was, 'I don't want to come into church. It makes me feel sad. The only time I've been is for my Grandad's funeral.' On these occasions we need to ensure that any visit to our churches is positive, warm (in at least two ways!) and fun. Thankfully, this youngster left the service with a smile on his face, and hopefully he now no longer equates church (and maybe God) with death.

CASE STUDY: Chill'n Chat

As part of the Schools Project's work in Laughton we started lunchtime clubs called Chill'n Chat. The clubs were initially aimed at those in year seven (first year secondary) to help them settle into their new school. The format of the session was to provide board games for the young people to play while they ate their lunch, and for the volunteers to chat with them – about schools, family or anything that came up. At the end of the session, the 'God-slot' was introduced, but always with the opportunity for youngsters to leave at that point – they rarely did! During the first year of the Project older pupils also wanted to attend, so other similar groups were established for them.

Some of the volunteers who worked in these groups were retired and would never have imagined themselves working with young people. However, because they were the age of some of the young people's grandparents, some good relationships were developed and the young people shared quite openly about what was happening in their lives. Other volunteers were older

Christian teenagers who were able to act as mentors and keep an eye out for them around the school. These young Christians began to take on leadership roles in the group, including leading the short 'God-slot'. Often something of the gospel was shared using drama or activities, and a question box was used which gave pupils an opportunity to ask questions anonymously about any aspect of faith. This is where the question at the beginning of this chapter appeared, along with others such as:

> 'How come Mary had a baby and she was a virgin?'
> 'Why did God make some animals evil? Why did God make some people evil?'

The question box developed into a significant part of Chill'n Chat, as it provided the young people with opportunities to ask questions in a 'safe' and anonymous way. In this increasingly post-Christian society, many of these young people have nowhere else to ask them. This point is picked up by Martin Robinson, who refers to an unpublished survey into young people's attitudes to church, worship and faith. Because the young people were from non-churched backgrounds, they could not find answers (or even a place to ask their questions) in the home or at school. 'The impression was given by many pupils that the lack of any place in which profound questions could be safely raised had meant that the questions simply stopped.'[10]

> **'The question box developed into a significant part of Chill'n Chat, as it provided the young people with opportunities to ask questions in a 'safe' and anonymous way. In this increasingly post-Christian society, many of these young people have nowhere else to ask them.'**

The volunteers discovered that generally the young people were keen to ask specific questions, which gave them opportunity to be more specific in their responses, often speaking from personal experience of faith. It can be difficult to know how to be relevant but the question box enabled us to 'scratch where they were itching'.

The older Chill'n Chat groups provided opportunities for discussion and debate and for deeper relationships to be developed. As a result, some of the young people went on to attend deanery youth weekends and others got involved with the deanery musicals that were staged. However, the older groups were also more difficult to work with, because so many different needs were presented. Some of the young people came because they were lonely and/or being bullied. Others were genuinely seeking to find out more about Christianity, and some came along specifically to cause trouble.

At one school, there was a persistent group of six young people who constantly demanded attention and often made outrageous comments in order to shock. We sensed early on that this group had some serious questions and a desperate need for positive attention and acceptance. This provided us with a dilemma; we didn't want to reject them totally, because we believed that our calling was to model God's unconditional love to them, but we didn't want to condone the negative behaviour either, or allow their behaviour to stop others coming. We reluctantly had to ask them to leave on several occasions and banned them from the following week's session. The fact that they kept coming back and, when certain members of the group weren't there, actually asked serious questions about faith and God, showed that there was some spiritual searching going on.

THINKING IT THROUGH

- Before you embark on any schools work, find out what current links exist between your church and school: how many of the congregation are parents/grandparents of pupils? Who works at the school – School Meals Supervisors (dinner ladies!), teachers, cleaners? Build on these links and pray for all those connected with the school.
- Find out what the school's needs are – ask them! Find out what other churches/Christian groups are doing – there's no point duplicating what's already being done. A key word is partnership: with the schools and with other groups of Christians.

- Make a good first impression when you make initial contact – better still, get someone already connected to the school to introduce you to the Head Teacher. A letter from you followed by a phone call to arrange a meeting is also a good first step.
- In the Schools Project we found that some 'spin-off events' were successful in building on contacts made in schools. Examples include parties, youth services, youth weekends and church youth groups. However, it's important to be 'up-front' if the event will include overt Christian content. We shouldn't get young people to an event under false pretences: they won't appreciate being manipulated – but then, who does?
- We also found that there was still too big a gap between the churches and the young people in schools. It is important to recognize that the majority of young people worked with in school may never become part of traditional church congregations; the cultures are just too different. Their youth groups often become church for them instead, because they relate more accurately to their needs and culture. It's worth asking about the implications of this where churches are supporting schools work financially and expect their congregations to increase as a result.
- Some other opportunities for practical involvement in schools can also include:

    Supporting the Parent Teacher Association (or starting one!)
    Helping with music, drama, etc.
    Praying for your local school
    Having a regular schools' prayer slot in church services
    Developing mentoring programmes or supporting those that already exist.

CLASS ACT

SUMMARY

I am more convinced than ever of the importance of Christian work with schools. The opportunities are there but we are more reluctant to offer our involvement than the schools are to receive it! Don't be fearful but take advantage of the links you may already have with a school and build on them. Hopefully this chapter has provided some pointers towards good practice, but talk to teachers you know and use the resource list if you are unsure of how to approach this vital work.

An extensive list of ways to support schools can be found in:

Radford, Rowe and Baker, *Generation to Generation: Building bridges between churches and schools*, SU/Fanfare For a New Generation, 1999.
David Lankshear, *Churches Serving Schools*, Church House Publishing, 2002 (2nd edition).

People Resources

School head teachers and Christian teachers already in the Church don't bite! They are normally happy to explain what issues schools are facing and how they might be supported.

Each Anglican diocese has an education department that can offer information, news and resources.

Scripture Union employs field workers who are experienced in schools work and often offer support and training – www.scriptureunion.org.uk

Useful books

P. Brierley, *Steps to the Future Christian Research*, SU, 2000. Helpful statistics to appreciate the significance of schools work.
M. Robinson, *The Faith of the Unbeliever*, Monarch, 1994. Good introduction to factors concerning ministry in a post-Christian context.
Phil Wason, *Just Think About That!* SU, 1997. Outlines for secondary assemblies; I've also adapted them for short 'God-slots' in Chill'n Chat.
E. Williams, *The Schools Work Handbook*, SU, 1996. Practical guide to working in schools.

The Education Reform Act can be found at www.opsi.gov.uk
It's Your Move, SU, 2006. A book for Year 6s (top juniors) to help them in the transition to secondary school. There is also a teacher's pack.

More information on the Scripture Union web site – www.scriptureunion.org.uk/re-source/: This site has helpful resources designed for those running (or thinking about running) Christian groups in seconday schools.

www.assemblies.org: A really useful site of primary and secondary assembly outlines.

7 A LIGHT IN THE DARKNESS? Nightclub chaplaincy

Diana Greenfield

INTRODUCTION: Clubbing together

Nightclub chaplaincy is an area of exciting, growing and innovative ministry. As a location for ministry the nightclub can offer many opportunities that other environments don't. People from many different backgrounds and cultures come together to socialize, dance and drink. Most will go clubbing for either enjoyment or escapism, and the chaplaincy service aims to be God's hands, feet, ears and mouth to bring the gospel into an environment that is often perceived, by outsiders, as a den of iniquity.

This chapter is based on my own experience of working in Norwich, Bournemouth and now Maidstone. The aim is to explore the role of the nightclub chaplain and to give some practical pointers for those who want to get involved in this form of ministry.

CASE STUDY: God on the dance floor

Jane is a regular in one of the nightclubs in town. Normally she likes a couple of drinks and a dance with her mates on a weekend. One week she turns up in the club on a Tuesday night. She is already quite drunk and continues to knock back the drinks. By 12.30 am she is found hugging the toilet and being sick as a result of the amount of alcohol she has consumed. The doormen take her to the first aid room and call the chaplain. Jane is clearly upset and not her usual life-loving self. As the chaplain sits with her, Jane tearfully explains that her mum has recently died and she is struggling to come to terms with her loss. Jane has no one who can help her make sense of what has happened.

> 'As the chaplain sits with her, Jane tearfully explains that her mum has recently died and she is struggling to come to terms with her loss. Jane has no one who can help her make sense of what has happened.'

On the same night one of the team is approached by someone who wants to know what the word 'Chaplain' means on the back of the T-shirt they are wearing. A brief explanation from the team member prompts the young person to enter into a conversation about their own experiences of church from childhood and their current spiritual beliefs. The young person was brought up in a Christian family and had been made to go to church twice every Sunday until they were 16. They had resented this and had been subject to a lot of ridicule from peers. Despite all this, the young person still has a strong Christian faith but tells the team member that they don't feel they need to go to church to be a Christian.

THE ISSUE: Going where young people go

The two incidents described above are typical of what can be encountered by a nightclub chaplain. Nightclubs are an untapped mission field. Each week, thousands of young people aged 18–25 go there to socialize. Much of the time they are simply there for a good time: a chance to go out with friends, a few drinks and a dance. However, some young people who are struggling to handle a situation in their lives may turn to clubbing, or one of the many vices the club culture offers, as a form of escapism.

In the UK, a few churches and organizations have started chaplaincy work in nightclubs. The web sites of some examples can be found in the resources list at the end of this chapter. But what are Christians doing in what some might regard as 'dens of iniquity'?

Nightclub chaplaincy usually involves a team of volunteers going into the local nightclub(s) and being available to anyone who needs to talk with someone who can listen, support, encourage and offer a tangible expression of the love of Jesus Christ. The team are identified by T-shirts which bear the word 'Chaplain' and are available in the club during opening hours as well as being prepared to have follow-up chats with those they meet. The permission and cooperation of the management of the club is, of course, essential.

The role of the nightclub chaplain is to be God's hands, ears, eyes and mouth in the nightclubs, meeting the needs of both clubbers and staff in whatever way possible. This can be anything from a listening ear if things are rough, to holding the bucket while someone is sick, or having an in-depth conversation with someone about their spiritual journey.

> 'The role of the nightclub chaplain is to be God's hands, ears, eyes and mouth in the nightclubs, meeting the needs of both clubbers and staff in whatever way possible. This can be anything from a listening ear if things are rough, to holding the bucket while someone is sick, or having an in-depth conversation with someone about their spiritual journey.'

The rest of this chapter explores some of the issues, challenges and practicalities involved in nightclub chaplaincy.

BACKGROUND: Understanding the opportunity

Nightclubs are a place where huge numbers of young people/adults can be found; in fact probably one of the few places other than educational establishments where such large numbers can be found all in the same place at the same time. It is a place where they will choose to relax and let off steam. Young people are also away from the supervision of parents, teachers or other authority figures, meaning that they are likely to drop their guard and chat about more intimate and personal issues. Although perhaps this is an obvious statement, it is important to remember that any ministry conducted in nightclubs is about entering the young people's space and this needs to be handled with sensitivity and respect.

It is very difficult to know how many clubs there are in the UK for a number of reasons. New nightclubs open and shut in towns all the time, they may have a name change or a new entrepreneur may decide to try his/her hand at running a nightclub. Even in Maidstone, where I am currently working, I will only ever say there are seven-ish nightclubs, because a new one may have opened or one closed that I haven't yet heard about. In Bournemouth, where I worked previously, there are around 30 nightclubs. The capacity of a nightclub can range from 5,000 in the Syndicate in Blackpool, which is currently the UK's largest nightclub, down to many venues with a capacity of 100–200. The smaller venues can cater for a more specialist music market or generate a more intimate atmosphere. In Maidstone the largest capacity club can take 1,800 people, but that will not always be full; across the seven-ish clubs, probably somewhere around 16,500 clubbers will be out during a week. The legal age to go clubbing is 18, in line with the UK drinking laws. However, there are some clubs who have an older minimum age, for example over-21s, to attract a different crowd.

If you asked a young person why they went clubbing, it is unlikely that they would respond that it met their spiritual needs. However, talk to a clubber about belonging to a community, or about the deep and touching experiences that they have encountered in some of the music they listen to in the club, and you start to realize that clubs are a place that offers some of the expressions of spiritual and community needs that we in the Church might be hoping to offer.

> 'Talk to a clubber about belonging to a community, or about the deep and touching experiences that they have encountered in some of the music they listen to in the club, and you start to realize that clubs are a place that offers some of the expressions of spiritual and community needs that we in the Church might be hoping to offer.'

A Christian response: the role of the nightclub chaplain
The role of the nightclub chaplain can be viewed from a number of different perspectives.

First, perhaps the all-encompassing role of the nightclub chaplain is to 'loiter with intent'. It is simply about being there to do whatever God is calling us to in any particular situation, whether that is dealing with the immediate and practical needs of the clubbers or having a deep discussion about belief which enables someone to travel a further step on their faith journey.

Secondly, and more specifically, it is about being a modern-day Good Samaritan. Often the first thing that the chaplain needs to do is meet the practical needs of someone who is drunk and probably out of control. This can be really basic, such as holding her hair out of her face while she is sick, helping the doormen get her to the first aid room, perhaps ensuring that her dignity is maintained as she is carried through the club. It is important that her friends are found and that a safe way of getting her home is arranged. These are all responsibilities that the chaplaincy can take on which go above and beyond the duties of a normal nightclub staff team.

Following on from this it could well be that as the individual leaves the club the chaplain hands her a contact number or looks out for her next time she is in the club to give her an opportunity to talk. Chaplains need to be able to offer a listening ear more than they need to be able to offer solutions to problems; they are often the first port of call. When a person is feeling vulnerable and their guard is down due to the effects of drugs or alcohol they will look for someone with whom they can talk. Having knowledge of the local counselling services, drug rehab, Crisis and Relate is extremely useful, also other services which may be specific to the area, for example a local youth support service.

The above describes only half of what being a nightclub chaplain is about. If all chaplains ever do is to pick up the pieces of what is going on in people's lives, then they are really only glorified social workers. The other side of the coin is that this is a Christian ministry in an amazing mission field. Most current research would suggest that the young people of today have a deep awareness of things spiritual but aren't necessarily interested in inherited religion. Inherited religion or traditional religion is what young people are often taught in schools; they learn the language of religion but don't take part in the practice. Imagine that someone was taught the rules of football but was never given the opportunity to play the game. Similarly, when young people learn about religion they learn the rules but not how to live it. Consequently, when they want to express things in spiritual terms they resort to the language that they know to be associated with spiritual things, even if it doesn't mean quite the same to them as it would to regular churchgoers. Rather than trying to develop this theory any further at this point, Phil Rankin's research into young people and spirituality (*Buried Spirituality*) offers a clear and considered discussion, including many quotes from interviews with young people, of how they use the language of religion and spirituality in today's world. (Alison Booker's chapter in the final section of this book also explores the complexity of changing language in our mission to young people.)

The key issue with regard to the missionary role of the nightclub chaplaincy is how to walk the line between Christian culture and club culture without either denying our Christian values or alienating ourselves from the young people. Although I struggle when people think that nightclubs are dens of iniquity, it is true to say that many of life's most obvious temptations are on offer in most clubs. I would never look for the club culture to come to an end, but my hope is that the attentions of the clubbers would be turned to God. To be an effective Christian in the club culture clearly needs a strong faith, one where despite the temptations you can stand for something different. Over the years I have discovered that many people are challenged (often surprisingly so) simply by my integrity, and it is that which makes them ask more about faith.

> 'Over the years I have discovered that many people are challenged (often surprisingly so) simply by my integrity, and it is that which makes them ask more about faith.'

Ultimately Jesus Christ is the best that we can offer to anyone we meet wherever we are. As long as we are honest to ourselves, to God and to those we meet, we can present Jesus in a credible way for anyone in the nightclubs or at the gym or outside the chip-shop.

THINK IT THROUGH: Could it be for you?

Nightclub chaplaincy can be seen as the 'sexy' thing when it comes to mission and young people, but it takes hard slog, commitment and patience. If you are challenged to establish a ministry to the clubbers in your area, make sure you do your groundwork first.

Doing your homework

- First of all, you need to establish how many clubs there are in your town/city.

- Roughly how many young people in your area go clubbing in one week?
- What kind of clubs are they? Do they play specialist music and therefore attract a specific clientele, or is it a more 'cheesy' club that attracts a different type of clubber?
- Try finding out about other projects that you might be able to visit, or speak to the workers to get a clearer idea of some of the highs and lows of working in the club culture.
- The web sites listed at the end of this chapter may be good starting points.

Gaining the support of your church or organization

Gather key church leaders for an open discussion to find out how much support there may be for the project. Remember that a verbal acknowledgement of support can often be very different from those same people delivering support either in terms of money or people. You will also need to ensure that there will be more than adequate prayer support for the ministry. Often I have found that retired members of congregations very much value the ministry and want to pray when they don't feel able to get out and do it themselves. It will obviously be vital to communicate news about the project to your prayer supporters on a regular basis.

Approaching the club management

If you are planning to start a new ministry to a nightclub in your area it is likely to be far more effective if you have the support of the management of the club. A good relationship with the management ensures an open relationship with the staff, which can be extremely beneficial. A good door staff team will value what you are doing because it will take the pressure off them to look after the people who are simply intoxicated and return their attentions to deterring trouble.

Who will do the work?

Consider whether your project will be run and staffed by volunteers or whether you have the resources and desire to employ a full- or part-time worker. Even if a paid worker is in post, there is still room for a team of volunteers. The key thing to look for in volunteer team members is people with a heart to serve the clubbers. People can be taught how to share their faith, how to be sensitive in the way they listen to people and how to look out for the clubbers who might need their service. Their passion for the gospel, which they share, and the love of God that they are there to express needs to come from God; otherwise, in my experience, they are likely to lack commitment and loyalty to the project or to run out of steam.

Think through your follow-up

Be prepared for people from the clubs to want to visit churches or to explore Christianity. Just as in any form of missionary work, it is important that follow-up opportunities are in place to disciple those who want to make a commitment to Christianity, whether that is by simply being prepared to accompany someone to a church service or by establishing some sort of forum for them to meet with others who are exploring the Christian lifestyle.

There may be implications for the form of services currently run by your church. Would young people fit in? Or do you need to consider changing the style of service, or starting a new service entirely, to cater for their needs, e.g. a café church, or club-style worship?

> **'There may be implications for the form of services currently run by your church. Would young people fit in? Or do you need to consider changing the style of service, or starting a new service entirely, to cater for their needs, e.g. a café church, or club-style worship?'**

Be in it for the long haul . . .

Remember that nightclub ministry is mission at home. It is something that takes passion, and commitment for the long haul. It takes time to win respect from the clubs and their staff and for the reputation of the project to become known and appreciated. It also takes time to find the right people to serve on the team. Don't give in to the temptation to rush!

A LIGHT IN THE DARKNESS?

SUMMARY

Mission to young people in the nightclubs is, in many ways, no different to ministering to young people anywhere else, whether that be the skate park, or the local youth club. The big difference is that there are substances and/or alcohol available and as a result the young people may be especially vulnerable.

Clubbers are often extremely spiritually aware, but it is important to be patient and to see the work as long-term. It can be intensely frustrating to have an amazing conversation with someone one night and explain the gospel to him or her, and yet next week they will come back and say they have visited a Buddhist meditation centre. Remember that mission is us working with God, who is already doing his work in his time. If we have a team of pray-ers whose key responsibility is to pray for those we meet and ask God to show himself to them, then we need to trust God with the outcomes of our work.

The nightclubs are a place where we sow the seeds of the gospel. We may never see much fruit from it but we don't know what trees might grow from those seeds in 20 years' time.

A LIGHT IN THE DARKNESS?

Unsurprisingly there is very little written about nightclub chaplaincy, but there are some useful web sites:

www.nightclubchaplain.co.uk
This is the web site for the Maidstone nightclub chaplaincy project in which I am involved.

www.clubchaplain.co.uk
This is the web site for Bournemouth Nightclub Chaplaincy.

www.freshexpressions.org.uk
Keep an eye on this web site, which has one or two references to nightclub ministries around the country.

www.emergingchurch.org
This is a great web site for those who are considering church for today's young people.

http://jonnybaker.blogs.com
Jonny's blog has some good links for club ministry and emerging church information.

I would advocate reading books by Brian McLaren such as *A New Kind of Christian* (Jossey Bass Wiley, 2001) and *Generous Orthodoxy* (Zondervan, 2006).

To understand more about young people and spirituality try *Buried Spirituality* by Phil Rankin (Sarum College Press, 2005).

A book that I often give to people whose self-esteem is very low is Brennan Manning, *The Ragamuffin Gospel* (Multnomah Publishers, 2005). It is a fantastic way of presenting grace, God's unconditional love, through the life of the author.

And I have no qualms about giving away copies of the Bible, but I look for contemporary translations and tend to point them towards reading Luke. The Contemporary English Version/The Message or the Street Bible all work well.

Happy clubbing!

8 IGNORANCE IS BLISS? Young Christians living in a multi-faith society

David Booker

INTRODUCTION

Britain today is a richly mixed society where many faiths and beliefs are followed. However, most youth group programmes do little or nothing to help equip their young people to understand the faith of others or the implications of living as a Christian in a multi-faith society. Is this ignorance really bliss? This chapter argues that ministers and youth leaders can no longer bury their heads in the sand. If we are going to answer God's call to mission in the UK today we must learn what it means to love our neighbours from other faith communities.

THE ISSUE

Since the tragic events at the World Trade Center on 11 September 2001 there has been wide debate about what it means to live in a kaleidoscope society of many beliefs, faiths and cultures. How do we recognize diversity while combating exclusion? What are our universal rights and responsibilities to each other regardless of faith or cultural differences and where (if anywhere) should the limits on personal choice and expression be drawn? At its heart this question asks what sort of society we want to live in. Or, perhaps more properly for Christians, what sort of society God desires.

For Christians, although the Bible lays out principles, it does not deliver a simple, neat answer to this question. Indeed, some Old Testament passages, where God commands Moses and others to wipe out those standing in the way of his people, appear to modern readers as no more than religiously motivated genocide. Add to this theological problem the ignorance of most Christians about the faith and practices of other religions and the current climate of fear and suspicion between so-called western and Islamic cultures, and it is no wonder that those working with young people totally avoid the issue. Many wonder whether, if they did dare to begin addressing these issues, parents or their wider church would support them.

When I first left school I took a gap year, some of which was spent in inner-city Birmingham. For the first time I was faced with a number of issues, including how I responded to those from other faith communities, an interest I have kept to this day. When I became Diocesan Youth Officer for Leicester I was delighted to be able to have a limited involvement in some of the groups working to increase understanding between faith communities. However, I was amazed at the reaction of many of my friends on hearing I was involved in these groups. Having in the past worshipped and worked in large evangelical churches, I thought my evangelical friends were pretty sure I was 'sound'. However, the wave of comments, often fuelled by suspicion, ignorance, fear, racism and arrogance, left me shocked and disappointed. How ironic that the part of the Church most noisily proclaiming the need to win others for Christ often becomes the least likely to engage practically with those from other faith communities at a personal level. It seems so disappointing that those who loudly proclaim their confidence in the gospel during the sermon in practice seem afraid to encourage their young people to step out of the safe church space they inhabit.

Authentic Christian mission involves a call to love, serve and witness to the whole world, including those of other faith communities. If our love for others does not overcome our suspicion, racism and fear we will never equip our young people to fulfil their call to mission.

> **'Authentic Christian mission involves a call to love, serve and witness to the whole world, including those of other faith communities. If our love for others does not overcome our suspicion, racism and fear we will never equip our young people to fulfil their call to mission.'**

THEORY: From changing hearts to shaking hands

Equipping young people to live as disciples in a multi-faith society is not an easy task. Before focusing on those whom we may regard as other, the first requirement is that we look honestly at ourselves. To put it bluntly, ignorant leaders cannot create informed young people. If leaders are not able to teach and discuss this area, they need to find others who can support them. There are good books, training packs and people available who are happy to help groups and leaders explore these areas (see the resources list). Of course some leaders are tempted to say 'It's not my problem', believing that unless they have visible groups of followers from other faiths in their local community they can ignore the issue. This naivety can leave our young people sorely unprepared for the issues they will face in dealing with other faiths. RE lessons will look at other faiths, the media will present the issues, and young people, who are naturally mobile, are almost bound to work or live alongside neighbours with other faiths at some point in their lives.

If living in a mixed community, any work the church does can potentially reflect its call to mission to all. However, often our entire 'mission' effort is implicitly only for those 'like us'. Loving others is easy to agree to in theory. Real love involves meeting and sharing. This meeting can take place formally through what are known as Dialogue Groups, specific groups set up with the intention of increasing understanding and awareness between different peoples of faith. Some time ago the British Council of Churches summarized the 'four principles of dialogue'.[1]

> **'Loving others is easy to agree to in theory. Real love involves meeting and sharing.'**

Dialogue begins when people meet each other
Ultimately, if we want to love our neighbours of other faiths we need to meet them. Often such meetings involve visiting each other's places of worship to gain an awareness of how faith is understood and practised. While another faith group remains 'they' it is easy to reject and ignore. Once we know followers of other faiths personally they become human beings who desire understanding and respect rather than caricatures. Too often in the Church those who begin thinking about these issues 'chicken out' of meeting those from other faiths in favour of inviting an expert to tell us about 'what they are like'!

Dialogue depends upon mutual trust and understanding
Welcoming others to your place of worship and sharing with them demands trust from both sides: a willingness to answer questions that may seem

strange without being defensive, and respecting the views and practices of others. This may mean covering your head or removing your shoes while visiting other places of worship without making a fuss, or it may mean being willing to apologize for the times the Church does get things wrong.

Dialogue makes it possible to share in service to the community

While we will disagree about many things, we shall also discover large areas of shared concerns where working together could make a real difference. Working together in a community to overcome issues of poverty, loneliness or social breakdown is working together on God's agenda. When we find ourselves working together with Hindu, Muslim or Sikh believers to clear up a local park, we may discover that we are building a little bit of God's kingdom together.

Dialogue becomes the medium of authentic witness

Dialogue does not mean pretending that we are all the same, or choosing to look only at those areas for which we share a common concern. As trust grows it becomes easier to talk about those areas where we disagree. In both agreements and disagreements, our meeting together provides followers of other faiths with an opportunity to learn about the difference our faith makes. As we share, explain and work together we are witnessing to our faith. If we take seriously the truth that mission is God's work, in which he invites us to join, then we will know that we can trust him with the results.

NEED TO KNOW: The two-sided coin of service and witness

There is a regular argument in the Church about whether our call to serve those of other faiths, because they often represent socially, economically or politically excluded groups, is of greater or lesser importance than our need to share faith with them. This debate, while taking much energy, fails to understand properly the connection between these two areas.

Effective faith sharing and effective social action have always been most successful when seen as two sides of the same coin. At its most simple, if our words and actions do not match, neither will be taken seriously. However, witnesses with dirty hands from practical service earn the right to speak and be listened to. A mistaken belief that our call is simply to convert those who have another faith is as narrow and unlikely to succeed as a simple understanding that only social care for those in need is required. Mission demands both responses from the believer.

> **'Effective faith sharing and effective social action have always been most successful when seen as two sides of the same coin. At its most simple, if our words and actions do not match, neither will be taken seriously.'**

Some people argue that any attempt to share Christianity with those from other faiths is imperialistic and wrong. According to this argument, we should simply devote our efforts to winning back lapsed Christians and leave other people to themselves. While this understanding may come from a laudable aim and be a response to the excesses of the past, it fails to take seriously the demand on followers of Jesus to share the faith and make disciples of all nations. While we must do all our evangelism with appropriate sensitivity and concern, we must not fall into an unwitting racism that excludes those of other faiths from the good news we have understood. At its most simple, if the Celtic Saints had followed this view on reaching Britain they would have sailed away again, leaving us following the Druids. While various New Age followers and modern Druids might welcome this, I will be forever grateful that they stayed and shared the truth of Christ with us.

What about schools?

Inevitably, some people will read this and feel that schools should be educating young people about world faiths rather than the Church. Of course schools do the best they can, but their focus tends to be on religious festivals and the practices of different faiths, often from an angle that seeks to find similarities rather than understand the differences. There is a real danger that what schools end up doing is creating a false divide between those with faith and those seemingly without it. Schools will not teach Christian young people to stand up for and be proud of their faith, nor will they teach how such a faith can effectively be shared with others. If we in the Church don't cover these important things, no one else is going to step in to do it for us. I want to see young people able to share their faith with confidence, not be undermined by those better educated about Christianity than they are themselves! We cannot love a neighbour we do not know and we cannot sit back and hope schools will do the job for us.

> **'I want to see young people able to share their faith with confidence, not be undermined by those better educated about Christianity than they are themselves! We cannot love a neighbour we do not know and we cannot sit back and hope schools will do the job for us.'**

CASE STUDY

The leaders of a large youth group in the south-west of England decided to introduce its group members to some of the various faiths and worldviews they would meet when they left the quiet, almost entirely white, market town. After much planning the young people arrived for an evening where various rooms had been set out as if they were the places of worship of various faiths. Being at least 20 miles from the nearest place of worship for a non-Christian faith, these rooms were as authentic as was practically possible. On entering each room the young people were treated as if they were really in the place of worship and had practices, beliefs and customs explained to them before having the opportunity to ask questions. It was an interactive and challenging evening that opened a new world to many of those taking part and helped them to think in a new way about their own faith. That evening took place over 20 years ago. Whether the leaders knew it or not, their work was having a great impact week by week. Twenty plus years on, I know that particular evening was important, because I was one of those young people. Little did they or I know then that 20 years later that evening would still be bearing fruit.

However unprepared or ill equipped the leaders felt, they still believed that this was an issue they needed to tackle. It was a risk, but I hope my experience of it shows that it was a step of faith well worth taking.

THINKING IT THROUGH: Doing the possible

How could your young people engage with those from another faith community? If a dialogue meeting sounds a rather ambitious involvement for your group, why not invite a faith leader to your group to answer questions and explain their faith? A little preparation in order to think through questions can make for an informative session that will not only help young people to learn but also to reflect on their own faith.

If not why not?

You may feel that thinking about these issues is not relevant to your group. Before you dismiss the idea, ask yourself why. Even if your young people have no contact with other faith communities now, they are likely to in the future in education or the world of work. Be honest with yourself about any underlying fears or concerns you may have about this area.

More committed than us?

Whenever I meet young Muslims or Sikhs I find myself challenged by both their level of commitment and their knowledge not only about their own faith but often about Christianity as well. Any journey into dialogue is likely to involve humbly recognizing that whatever we think about the faith of others, they are highly committed and devout. I know that I often feel that my own faith is poorly lived out by comparison. It is also challenging to see the resources that other faith groups put into training their young people. Jewish groups in particular stand out as investing heavily in their youth, especially in spending money to facilitate visits both to Israel and to the sites of concentration camps.

How well would your young people be able to defend the doctrine of the Trinity?

If they are discussing their faith with young Muslims it won't be long before the subject comes up! Of course we need to respond with humility and grace, but we also need to teach our young people how to defend their faith intellectually. As Christians we are not always good at teaching our young people to think for themselves and understand why our faith looks the way it does. Shying away from tough questions won't do. We need the confidence to handle doubts, fears and tough areas head on without being ashamed. If we keep our young people wrapped up in cotton wool we do them no favours when it comes to living out their faith in the world.

Anyone know where the Christians are hiding?

A constant frustration for those who work in the area of dialogue and understanding is that it is always easier to find Muslim, Jewish or Hindu

> **'Shying away from tough questions won't do. We need the confidence to handle doubts, fears and tough areas head on without being ashamed. If we keep our young people wrapped up in cotton wool we do them no favours when it comes to living out their faith in the world.'**

young people to participate in groups or meetings than young Christians. How will young followers of other faiths ever understand authentic Christianity unless there are committed young people who are willing to meet with them face to face and show them what living by faith in Christ means? From the way that some leaders wrap up their young people to avoid contamination, it can appear that there is little confidence in the Christian gospel. I am not sure whether the lack of encouragement for young Christians to be involved in this area comes from fear or from lack of love, but it surely cannot come from faithfully following the call of God to mission. We should be there witnessing and serving if we are to be faithful to our calling.

IGNORANCE IS BLISS?

SUMMARY

It is easy to fall into the trap of thinking that understanding other faith communities means only understanding Muslims. This is far from the case, but good resources which look at other faith communities are few and far between. Talk to your diocesan adviser and see what they can offer. Even better, invite a guest from another faith and let them share and answer questions!

God's call to mission demands that we lose our ignorance of other faiths. To fulfil the call on us to love, serve and witness to the world, we must be open to all regardless of faith or belief systems. We must be willing to face our own indifference, prejudice and fear, often in repentance, if we are to build the next generation of mission-focused disciples. If we fail in this call, we fail not only our wider society but also ourselves and ultimately, of course, God. It is time for those who work with young people to take their collective head out of the sand and begin to address these issues appropriately. When we do this we shall inevitably be misunderstood and sometimes rejected by our own. That is the cost of following a crucified and risen Saviour into the world he redeemed.

IGNORANCE IS BLISS?

Most Anglican dioceses have some form of adviser in faith relations who can provide support, advice, resources, training and contacts to help explore this area more fully. However, here is a good list for starting out.

Books

Probably one of the easiest reads, which gives a good understanding of all the major world faiths, is *The New Lion Handbook of World Religions* (Lion, 2005).

Christine A. Mallouhi, *Waging Peace on Islam* (Monarch, 2000) is a long but very informative read.

Andrew Wingate, *Celebrating Difference* (Darton, Longman & Todd, 2005) is a careful study of some of the big issues involved in relating to those of other faiths. Guaranteed to give you plenty to think about!

For adults CMS produces *The Dialogue Pack*, 'A four-part study pack designed to support Christians in understanding and relating to Muslims and Islam' (more details at www. cms-shop.org.uk). With a little adaptation this resource can also work well with young people.

Internet resources

www.peacemakers.tv

A growing web site from the Christian charity Feed the Minds. Lots of great, high-quality resources and ideas. Well worth a look at!

The Connect Pack from www.interfaith.org.uk has good information and lots of links to help and advice.

Organizations

The St Philip's Centre is rooted in the multi-faith context of Leicester and is a national ecumenical training centre under the Presence and Engagement initiative of the Church of England. It provides training for Christians, those of other faiths and civic partners. It enables Christians and churches to be a confident presence in a multi-faith world, prepared to share their own faith and learn from others. The Centre is being developed by the Anglican Diocese of Leicester, St Philip's Church, the Methodist, United Reformed and Roman Catholic churches. Baptists are also part of the Steering Group. www.stphilipscentre.co.uk

The Intercultural Leadership School brings together young people from different faith communities to learn leadership and conflict resolution skills together. Successful schools have run in Bradford and Leicester, with plans for more to happen across the UK. More details of the work of ICLS around the world can be found at www.intercivilization.net

9 FEELING THE HEAT: Engaging young people in environmental issues

Martyn Lings

INTRODUCTION: Change is here

The majority of scientists now agree that climate change is occurring and many governments are committed to lowering pollution, preventing global warming and conserving biodiversity. We know that many young people are passionately concerned to see changes in the way we treat our world, but how often do you hear a sermon on why God wants us to care for the environment and recycle? This chapter explores the link between young people's concern about environmental change and their faith. In doing so it grapples with the meaning of the fifth Mark of Mission: to strive to safeguard the integrity of creation, to sustain and renew the life of the earth.

THE ISSUE: Can young people relate their environmental concern to their faith?

Young people are often more concerned than the Church in general about the environment. To enable them to link their faith with their concern for creation, leaders need to understand why the environment matters so much and how faith connects to it.

David King, the UK government's chief scientific adviser, stated that 'Climate change is the most severe problem that we are facing today, more serious even than the threat of terrorism.'[1] On first reading this statement may seem rather extreme; surely climate change can't be as dangerous as someone planting a bomb on a crowded bus?

But then consider that the World Meteorological Organization[2] has reported that we are now experiencing record numbers of extreme weather events, such as tornados, hurricanes, droughts and floods that have caused thousands of deaths and millions of pounds' worth of destruction. The respected scientific research organization Conservation International[3] has stated that the world stands to lose up to 750 plant and animal species within the next 10 to 50 years. What's more, the population groups that are going to be hit the hardest are those in developing countries, with likely increases in drought in Africa and increased flooding in low-lying countries like Bangladesh. Considering climate change in this light, David King's statement becomes far less extreme and actually quite plausible, and he is just referring to climate change, which makes up only a part of the devastation that we are wreaking upon the planet. Put simply, the environment is taking a hammering and the longer the beating goes on the less likely it will ever recover.

We are all aware of environmental action groups. The likes of Greenpeace, the World Wildlife Fund (WWF) and the Royal Society for the Protection of Birds (RSPB) are household names. However, few could name a Christian conservation group or any direct involvement of the Church with environmental protection. As concern for the environment became more prominent in the late 1960s and early 1970s it was pockets of secular society that led the charge for conservation. The Church, as an organization, did not appear to be involved with the issue. More recently the Church has started to embrace environmental issues with the inclusion of the sustaining of creation in the Anglican Consultative Council's mission statement for churches[4] and the Church of England's Shrinking the Footprint campaign,[5] as part of which Archbishop Rowan Williams made the strong statement that

> For the Church of the 21st century, good ecology is not an optional extra but a matter of justice. It is therefore central to what it means to be a Christian.

This stance is also echoed in *Sharing God's Planet*, a recent report on the environment from the Church of England's Mission and Public Affairs Council. But these good official attitudes are only slowly filtering down to many local churches.

One of the main reasons that Christians have not been involved in environment issues is a theology that saw conservation of the earth as irrelevant. This leads to questions and comments such as:

'If we have eternal life in heaven why do we need to care for what happens here?'

'I thought that the whole world was going burn up at the end of time anyway so why bother?'

'Jesus came to save people not plants didn't he?'

'God has given us dominion over the earth so our use of it is justified.'

'Where in the Bible does it say that we should care for the creation?'

However, slowly things are changing. Even in the United States, a country where the government and churches are not known for their environmental concern, there are signs of a changing attitude. Although our young people will probably be asking what took the Church so long!

THEORY/BACKGROUND TO THE ISSUE

When considering the question of what the environment has to do with Christianity it is inevitably to the Bible and Jesus that we first turn. In this section we will look at a few key passages that will give us a clear answer. However, it should be noted that the whole Bible is packed with references to the value that God places on his creation.

Let us first look at how God views his creation. In Genesis 1.31 we read that 'God saw all that he had made, and it was very good' (NIV). When reading the story of Noah we note that God chooses to save two of every species, not just humans, and when he makes his new covenant in Genesis 8 and 9 it is with mankind and every living creature. Furthermore, in Job 38–41 we find God demonstrating his intimate and loving relationship with his earth in an extended discourse with Job. So we know that God thinks his creation is great. In fact he values it so highly that even when things go wrong he still repairs and conserves it and promises never to destroy it.

Now let's turn to the instructions that God has given us for how to treat this earth that he loves so much. When God created human beings we learn that one of his first intentions was that we should 'rule over' (NIV), or have dominion over, all living creatures (Genesis 1.28). The use of the word 'dominion' has led some to hold the opinion that we can therefore dominate the earth in whatever ways serve our purposes. However, this is a serious error. As Christians we should be trying to follow Christ and be more like him (God the Son) in all that we do. Therefore in order to understand the word, we should be asking how God exercises his dominion over us. Then we can try to imitate his example. In Philippians 2 we read that Jesus came to love and serve. Therefore, if we are trying to model God's example of how to exercise dominion, we should be doing the same, not using the word 'dominion' as an excuse to exploit God's creation for our own selfish gain.

> **'In Philippians 2 we read that Jesus came to love and serve. Therefore, if we are trying to model God's example of how to exercise dominion, we should be doing the same, not using the word 'dominion' as an excuse to exploit God's creation for our own selfish gain.'**

Another clue to the nature of our 'dominion' is found in Genesis 2.15, where God calls Adam to 'work' (*abad*) and 'care' (*shamar*) for the Garden of Eden. The Hebrew words *abad* and *shamar* can be accurately translated as 'to serve' and 'to keep or protect'. So conservation was actually one of the earliest commandments God gave us!

Finally, in Genesis 2.19 God brings every creature before the man so that he can name them. This is a significant act that demonstrates a close relationship, intimate knowledge and a level of care between man and the rest of creation.

You may have heard people ask why we should care for the earth when we are going to heaven when we die; others say that in 2 Peter 3.10 it states that the earth is going to be laid bare, destroyed or burned up, so why should we try and conserve it? To answer these questions we need to look at God's intention for redeeming his fallen creation. Central to Christian belief is the understanding that God created the world in perfect relationship with himself. As a result of the fall our relationship has become broken. This fracture includes our relationship with God, other people, and the rest of creation. We are no longer fulfilling our role as stewards and servants of creation as God intended;

we are not imitating God as we should be. This is why we read in Colossians 1.16-20 that Christ created all things, he holds all things together and through him all things will be restored and reconciled and redeemed. Jesus' redeeming work heals our relationship with God, each other and the rest of creation.

The implication of this is that we are called us to continue his redeeming work. We are to work towards healing and redemption in all creation.

> 'We should care for creation because it is part of the mission that God has set for us in his plan to redeem the earth.'

It may be obvious how we do this with people, but how do you carry out Jesus' work with a forest? Simple: just follow the original instructions that God gave us in Genesis; follow God's own pattern for creation by ruling over creation with love and care, serving and protecting it. So, to answer the first question, we should care for creation because it is part of the mission that God has set for us in his plan to redeem the earth.

In response to the second question, a better translation and understanding of 2 Peter 3.10 seems to be that the earth will be 'found' or 'discovered' rather than laid bare and destroyed and the reference to fire is describing a refining fire. Adding weight to this argument is 2 Peter 3.13, where we read about the promise of new heavens and new earth. The word 'new' in this verse translates the Greek word *kainos*, which means 'renewed' rather than 'brand new'. So the picture we get is of a renewal of the earth. If this is God's intention, then it makes more sense to understand 3.10 within this context as well, suggesting that after a refining and purifying fire the earth and everything in it will be found or discovered.

Finally, another reason why we should care for the environment comes in Psalms 24 and 104, where it says that the 'the earth is the Lord's, and everything in it' (Psalm 24.1) and that in his wisdom he made it all (Psalm 104.24). If we understand the meaning of these words, we realize that we are fools to think that it's a good idea to destroy something that belongs to God, which he made in his infinite wisdom!

NEED TO KNOW: So what can we help young people do?

So now that we are clear about why we should be trying to prevent environmental destruction, let's get on and do something. But what can we do to encourage young people to respond to this great need? Well, the answer is really quite a bit. If everyone changed their lifestyle a little, the impact would be huge; and if you're thinking 'Yeah, but I bet most people won't bother', then remind yourself that as Christians we don't stop helping those in need just because most other people don't bother. When carrying out 'environmentally friendly' action we are truly serving and worshipping God.

Below are some of the things that you can encourage individual young people to do; and other actions that can be done by groups of people like a youth group, school or church.

Recycle

This is probably the action that people think of first. Thankfully, a lot of councils now provide recycling as part of their rubbish collecting service. We should encourage young people to make sure that their households recycle, ensuring that everything is put in the right location. All packaging should indicate whether it can be recycled. If you're not one of the lucky ones with a recycling council, don't despair; simply track down your local recycling centre by contacting your local council through an email or phone. The key to getting started with recycling is to be organized: set up a series of boxes in your kitchen or somewhere handy, one for each material; then you'll constantly be reminded and it will become a regular pattern of life.

Buy green energy

You have no doubt heard all about renewable energy, and how it currently only makes up a tiny percentage of our national energy output. Well, the best way to change this is to make sure that your home is supplied with renewable energy. Yes, you can do this! In the UK companies such as 'Good Energy' will provide your house with only renewable energy. Not only is this straight away better for the environment but it will also encourage future investment in renewable energy. Why not encourage young people to speak to their parents about this?

Walk or cycle

Yep, its time to build up those muscles. Using cars around town on short trips is highly uneconomical and creates a lot more pollution per mile than driving on a motorway. Both leaders and young people should consider walking or cycling to your youth group and other nearby places instead . . . you know it makes sense!

Compost

Sounds strange? How will rotting vegetables save the planet? Simple: by reducing household waste we can decrease the number of habitats that are ripped up and degraded to make landfill sites, and also lower the number of dustbin truck trips, which all burn oil and are needed to clear away our rubbish.

Lights out

This is the easiest of all. Turn off unused lights, including LEDs, and use energy-saving bulbs. It is estimated that if we all turned off the LEDs in our houses, such as the ones that indicate that the TV's on standby, it would save an amount of energy equivalent to a whole power station. How many of your young people leave things on standby or keep things charging when the battery is full?

> **'It is estimated that if we all turned off the LEDs in our houses, such as the ones that indicate that the TV's on standby, it would save an amount of energy equivalent to a whole power station.'**

Green churches and schools

Find out whether your young people's church or school recycles, uses energy saving light bulbs and is signed up to a green energy provider. If they don't or aren't, then keep pestering them!

Carbon neutral people

Organise a carbon neutral church service or youth group meeting by getting the congregation or youth group members and their parents to pay for the CO_2 they produce by driving to church through supporting an organization such as 'Climate Stewards'. Such organizations will offset their carbon emissions through tree planting and other sustainable enterprises. The cost is fairly low and it is a good way of getting people on board with being accountable for their pollution. See www.climatestewards.org or www.climatecare.org for more details.

Volunteer

Get some of your youth group together and volunteer on a conservation project. You'll learn a great deal about the world we live in and how to look after it – and have lots of fun too. There are quite a few organizations that do this, including Christian ones like A Rocha.

CASE STUDY

A Rocha is an international conservation organization with a twist: it is Christian. It works from a perspective that it is part of our mission as Christians to care for creation. Since its original establishment in Portugal over 20 years ago the group has spread all over the world and now has projects in 15 countries.

One such project is situated in Kenya on the east coast of Africa. Here the A Rocha team has set up a scheme that is a great example of how God's calls for us to care both for each other and for the rest of creation can work in tandem. The scheme, called the Arabuko-Sokoke Schools and Ecotourism Scheme (ASSETS), solves the dual problems of localized poverty and the destruction of rare and endangered habitats and species. The Arabuko-Sokoke forest and neighbouring Mida creek contain many globally threatened bird and mammal species and are considered one of the most important forests for threatened birds within mainland Africa. However, many species and habitats are now threatened by illegal hunting and logging and the pressure of the surrounding communities that use the forest for their daily needs. The illegal activities arise from the poverty of the local people. They have to hunt and to sell wood if they want to make enough money to survive, particularly if they want their children to go to school.

The ASSETS project works by channelling funds generated through ecotourism into providing eco-bursaries for local children so that they can afford to attend school. The benefit for the environment is that local people no longer need to exploit the forest to pay for schooling and they learn to value the forest because they benefit from it. The families involved in the scheme receive environmental education and are also provided with tree seedlings that they can grow and use for fuel and timber and also sell, thus reducing the need to illegally log the forest. The ASSETS programme is a great example of how environmental conservation goes hand in hand with caring for people and is a part of our Christian missionary work.

'The ASSETS programme is a great example of how environmental conservation goes hand in hand with caring for people and is a part of our Christian missionary work.'

THINKING IT THROUGH

Here are some questions to think about and use as discussion starters.

- We know that God loves us, but is he really bothered about a robin? Does he really care about what happens to the rest of the earth?
- Jesus told us to love God and love our neighbours, but why should we worry about caring for creation?
- Ask your group what they make of the following quotation: 'I agree that Jesus came to save us but I don't remember reading that the rest of creation is going to be saved too. Does the Bible say anything about whether the earth will be redeemed as well?'
- Use the following as a discussion starter: As Christians we are followers of Christ, but he didn't go around planting trees and composting, so why should we?
- Why has the Church done so little in the past to conserve the environment?
- Are people more important to God than the rest of creation?
- Since the advent of the environmental movement some environmentalists have blamed Christianity for the degradation of the earth. Some claim that the Church's indifferent opinion towards the environment has led to a general ambivalence within western society, in turn resulting in a lack of concern and care for the earth. Others maintain that Christianity was the key force that encouraged the development of science and technology and is therefore responsible for the damage that the new technology created. Is this fair criticism?

FEELING THE HEAT

SUMMARY

The earth is in a dire state. Species are disappearing at a faster rate than ever before in human history and our climate is beginning to change because of the pollution we are creating. If we don't change our behaviour towards our planet, then more people will die, starting with those in less developed countries, and then relatively soon it will cease to be able to support life. However, we know from the Bible that God loves his creation. He made it in his wisdom and is committed to repairing it when it goes wrong. God has called us to look after his creation in the same way that he looks after us, with a serving and loving attitude. Jesus came to redeem all creation, not just us, and he called us to carry on his redemptive work.

So, in conclusion, we all have a calling from God to care for the planet. We can all make a real difference, without necessarily having to live in caves and eat only cabbage and soya beans in order to do so!

FEELING THE HEAT

Shrinking the Footprint is the Church of England's national strategic campaign to enable its members and institutions to address – in faith, practice and mission – the pressing issue of climate change. It aims to challenge, encourage and support the whole body of the Church to shrink our environmental footprint. www.shrinkingthefootprint.cofe.anglican.org

Further reading on theology and the Christian call to care for creation

Mission and Public Affairs Council of the Church of England, *Sharing God's Planet*, Church House Publishing, 2005. Also includes an extensive bibliography.

Peter Harris, *Under the Bright Wings*, Regent College Publishing, 2000. The story of A Rocha's beginnings and why protecting and sustaining the environment is actually part of a holistic approach to mission.

Steve Bouma, *For the Beauty of the Earth*, Baker Academic, 2001. A study of the theological reasoning behind caring for creation. This also includes chapters concerning whether Christianity is to blame for the current environmental crisis.

R. J. Berry (ed.), *The Care of Creation*, IVP, 1994. A commentary by leading theologians and environmental experts on God's call to us to care for creation.

Web sites, many of which have areas and resources specifically for young people

www.arocha.org
The A Rocha International web site containing details of all A Rocha's work and providing everyday examples of Christians who are conserving the environment. A lot of environmental organizations provide volunteer opportunities. Enter 'environmental

or conservation volunteering' into a search engine and you'll find a stack of them. If you specifically wish to volunteer with a Christian conservation group, then currently A Rocha is the only option.

www.conservation.org
Conservational International is one of the leading scientific research and conservation organizations in this field. If you want to know more about the state of the earth's ecosystems and species then this is a good place to start.

www.climatewire.org
This web site collates the latest news articles and scientific research relating to climate change. It provides an easy way to stay in touch with the latest findings and research.

www.good-energy.co.uk
This web site tells you how to sign up for renewably generated electricity and has other handy energy-saving tips.

www.climatestewards.org.uk and www.climatecare.org
How to be Carbon Neutral. Groups such as Climate Stewards and Climate Care provide an online service through which you can compensate the carbon you create by driving your car or flying.

All the major conservation organizations, such as the World Wildlife Fund, Friends of the Earth, Greenpeace and the RSPB, also have sections within their web sites relating to the state of the environment.

10 SPARE CHANGE OR ALL CHANGE? Involving young people in issues of global poverty

Martin Parks

INTRODUCTION

> Three men in the United States have more money than the poorest 600 million people in the world.
>
> Poor countries pay back to rich countries more money than rich countries give in aid to the poor.
>
> 1.2 billion people – a fifth of the entire world – live on less than 60p a day.

You don't need a degree in global development or economics to understand that these statistics illustrate how great injustice in our world is. Young people take this to heart and in doing so express something of the heart of God for the poor. How we as leaders help them express their desire to change the world is a challenge we can too often overlook. Responding to poverty is, however, a key part of mission, as the third and fourth Marks of Mission clearly state:

> to respond to human needs by loving service;
> to seek to transform unjust structures of society.

THE ISSUE

I recently organized a stall at a large Christian youth event where we encouraged people to 'Vote With Their Feet'. By drawing around their shoes or feet they were joining a petition going to Tony Blair from people all over the country. This was a part of the Trade Justice Movement's 'Vote for Trade Justice' campaign. Over the two weeks hundreds of young people drew their feet, many of them taking the time to add a message to Tony Blair. Some were less than complimentary; others thanked Mr Blair for what he had already done and encouraged him to do more. Others were keen to understand more about meetings like the G8 and what they actually did. Having drawn around their feet, many asked 'What difference will this actually make?'

Young people, both Christian and other, are keen to engage with issues of global importance. While there may be much evidence to suggest that young people are losing interest in the political process, when it comes to issues of justice they are passionate and want to be involved. They see injustice as a 'black and white' issue. When every 3 or 4 seconds somebody somewhere dies of poverty, preventable diseases, or not having enough to eat, they see it for what it is: quite simply wrong. Something needs to be done about it now. Jesus encouraged his followers to become like children (Matthew 18.3) and in many ways we can learn from young people in recognizing what God's (and therefore our) attitude should be towards injustice and poverty.

One young guy came along to our stall at the youth event and sat down for twenty minutes just reading some of the resources on the stall. Finally he looked up at me from his place on the floor and said, 'This isn't fair, is it; God doesn't want the world to be this way, does he?' In that moment he had captured something of God's heart for the poor. His heart had been opened up to the reality of the world beyond the shores of comfortable England without travelling further than Shepton Mallet! He glimpsed the injustice and, with no deep theology or understanding of how global institutions govern our world, he understood how God felt about this situation. We are created in God's image and the things that trouble our hearts, trouble his also.

Young people are more than ready to be involved in the battle against poverty when they realize how preventable much of it is. This chapter will both give a theological understanding of why the issue of poverty matters and look at how young people can come to understand the experience of poverty better and begin taking action against it.

THEORY: Why should we care?

So much of the Bible sets out how we should approach poverty and the needs of others; how we can create and live within a just community. If you look for every passage from the Bible about the poor, wealth, poverty,

> **'We have created a Bible of holes by ignoring God's call to care for the poor.'**

injustice, the oppressed, you'll find thousands of verses on these topics. Jim Wallis tells a famous story of how he and a friend at university went through the Bible cutting out references to the poor. By the end their Bible was in ruins, falling apart in their hands. Jim Wallis took this battered Bible out when he preached, proclaiming to congregations that this is what we, in the rich western world, have done to the Bible. We have created a Bible of holes by ignoring God's call to care for the poor. Sadly, this has been reflected in the youth work in many churches, where global issues and challenging injustice have often fallen off the programme. If we fail to connect this issue to our young people, the pursuit of justice and a fairer world can often become a purely secular thing.

When we make this mistake we are missing out on a key part of the Christian faith and failing to express fully what it means to be ambassadors for God's kingdom in the here and now. Isaiah 58 clearly shows how being concerned for the poor and loving our neighbour draws us closer to God. It strengthens our faith and brings the light of God to the world around us. As Christians we are a people of hope. We should not be content to let the rich world continue on its path of greed and self-gratification, leaving a growing trail of increasing poverty behind it. We are called to be prophetic and speak up for those whose voice has been gagged, or who are so hungry that they don't have the strength to speak.

> **'As Christians we are a people of hope. We should not be content to let the rich world continue on its path of greed and self-gratification, leaving a growing trail of increasing poverty behind it. We are called to be prophetic and speak up for those whose voice has been gagged, or who are so hungry that they don't have the strength to speak.'**

Jesus modelled this prophetic call. His mandate was to tell good news to the poor, set the captives free, help the blind to see, free those who have been treated unfairly (Luke 4.18). He hung out with people that society considered the lowest of the low: so low, in fact that they were probably unnoticed. Jesus drew attention to their condition, healed them physically and challenged his followers to put them first. Jesus told stories to illustrate that whatever we do for the least in the world's eyes we are actually doing for him (Matthew 25.31-46). And of course Jesus told us to love our neighbour as ourselves.

When Jesus told his first followers to do this he was immediately asked, 'But who is my neighbour?' It is a question that has been echoed countless times down the ages and one that we need to find an answer to today: 'In this global village, who are our neighbours?'

Martin Luther King said: 'Before you've finished your breakfast this morning, you'll have relied on half the world.' It's true! If you think about where your pyjamas and clothes were made, where your toothpaste and soap come from, where your breakfast cereal, tea, coffee and fruit juice were grown, where your kettle, radio and shower were made, they have come from the four corners of the world to help you start your day.

Jesus told the story of the Good Samaritan to illustrate what it means to love our neighbour and his point was clear: when you see somebody in need, whoever they are, you need to respond by caring for them. Neither geographical location nor racial or religious choices define who our neighbour is. A person in need defines who our neighbours are. Many Christians respond to this call by raising money and supporting charities that use the money to directly help and support people in need. This is one great way of living out what it means to love our neighbour.

But imagine the story of the Good Samaritan continued. As he returned to pay the bills for the man he rescued and was travelling back down the road to Jericho he came across another man who had been attacked, robbed and left for dead by the side of the road. Again the Good Samaritan climbed down off his donkey and bandaged the injured man's wounds, placed him on his donkey and took him to the inn and placed him in the bed next to the first man. Again he told the innkeeper that he would return that way and pay any outstanding bills.

A week later the Good Samaritan was again travelling down that same road and again found a man lying half dead by the side of the road. By now his travel first aid kit was running out of plasters, but again he climbed down off his donkey, saw to to the injured man's needs, placed him on the donkey and took him to the inn. Imagine that this keeps happening again and again. Eventually it will come to a point where the Good Samaritan looks beyond the immediate need of the men he is rescuing from the road and seeks to understand what can be done to stop these men being attacked in the first place. Would better policing of the road help? Should the road be closed? How could he stop this injustice? When the situation becomes this bad we need to continue to care for the immediate need, but also to look beyond to the root cause of that need and see what can be done to stop people suffering.

This is what we need to do with global poverty. Giving money is a great start, but it is not enough. The issue is bigger than us being able to raise more money; we need to look at the root causes of poverty and do something about them.

> **'Giving money is a great start, but it is not enough. The issue is bigger than us being able to raise more money; we need to look at the root causes of poverty and do something about them.'**

NEED TO KNOW

One of the biggest causes of poverty, one that many of the NGOs such as Oxfam, Tearfund and Christian Aid are focusing on, is the way global trade takes place. It has been one of the key issues at the heart of the Make Poverty History campaign. Many of the everyday products we use come from some of the poorest places in the world. So, if we are buying so much from them and yet they still remain poor, there must be something fundamentally wrong.

Everybody understands the basics of trade: it's a simple case of buying and selling products and services. It takes place all over the world, from the huge sanitized malls and shopping centres of rich cities to the dusty markets found in every African town and village. But when that buying and selling is on a global scale and billions of pounds are being exchanged, it becomes a more daunting prospect. There are international organizations that provide laws and rules to govern the global market and supposedly help everyone get a fair deal.

Attempting to understand global trade is a huge task, but if we are going to get to the root causes of poverty then it's one we must learn something about. At the end of this chapter is a list of places where you can get much more information about international trade and some fun, interesting and provocative ways of encouraging young people to think about the issue. But for now here are a few statistics about global trade to start us thinking:

- International trade is worth $10 million a minute.
- But poor countries account for only 0.4 per cent of this trade. Since 1980 their share has halved.
- Rigged trade rules cost the developing world $700 billion a year, according to the UN.
- Income per person in the poorest countries in Africa has fallen by a quarter in the last 20 years.
- The prices of many poor countries' key exports are at a 150-year low.
- At one full meeting of the World Trade Organization, the EU had 500 negotiators. Haiti had none.
- After one round of trade negotiations, rich countries calculated that they would be $141.8 billion better off, while Africa would lose $2.6 billion.

CASE STUDIES

One exercise I have used on countless occasions to get people thinking about our global village, in youth work settings as well as in sermons, is to encourage everybody to look inside each other's clothes for the labels. Many, but not all, say which country they were made in. Have a globe or map of the world at the front and get everybody to place a post-it note or sticker on the country where her or his clothes were manufactured. Every time a sizeable proportion of the world is covered. And for those places not covered by our clothes, thinking about what people have eaten and drunk that day helps fill in the gaps. Chocolate made from cocoa beans from Ghana, coffee from Uganda or Brazil, bananas from the Caribbean and lamb from New Zealand. So much of what we depend on in this country comes from all around the world. Just in this simple exercise young people see that the term 'global village' is a very accurate one and realize that they are intimately connected with, or even depend on, the poor of the world.

One simple thing I have used in the past as a great way of introducing the injustice of international trade is the board game Monopoly. Many western governments and global financial institutions are promoting 'free trade' as a way of helping the poorest countries work their way out of poverty. It essentially encourages every nation to play the trading game by exactly the same rules, much the same as Monopoly. This, on the face of it at least, seems fair, the same rules for everyone. The reality is much different. If you imagine playing a game of Monopoly where your opponent started with hotels on Mayfair, Park Lane, the greens, reds and blues, the stations, the water works and electricity company and £5,000, and you had only Old Kent Road, £50 and a Get Out of Jail Free card, who'd win? Would it feel like a fair game to you? Although the game is 'fair' because the rules are the same for both of you, there will only be one winner. Now imagine if this wasn't just a game, but your livelihood depended on such a farcical system. The reality is quite scary and yet this is what is faced by millions of small-scale farmers around the world.

> **'If you imagine playing a game of Monopoly where your opponent started with hotels on Mayfair, Park Lane, the greens, reds and blues, the stations, the water works and electricity company and £5,000, and you had only Old Kent Road, £50 and a Get Out of Jail Free card, who'd win?'**

On a couple of occasions, when working with a smaller youth group, I have actually taken a game of Monopoly and divided up the properties and money unfairly and got the group to play the game. Most normal games of Monopoly finish in arguments and frustration, but when they start with unfairly distributed resources the reactions have been interesting to observe. Sometimes those with little don't want to play because they can see there will only be one winner. But if this were your livelihood there would be no way of backing out. On another occasion the poorer groups tried all sorts of creative ideas, working together to overcome the rich and powerful. But each time these schemes failed and the rich got richer, leaving the poor behind. The rich on the other hand have always failed to seek justice and have continued to develop their empires. Sometimes they would provide a small handout or ignore a small amount of rent owed to them, allowing the poor to continue in the game but never seeking to improve the poor player's condition.

It's a simple but very effective way of engaging young people with some of the feelings of powerlessness and frustration faced by many farmers around the world. It has often brought out real emotions of anger and bitterness towards the system and many young people have asked, 'If this is true, then what can we do about it?' It also shows young people that they are just as likely to want to hold on to their riches and powerful position as those who hold them in the real world. Seeking a fairer world will involve some form of sacrifice.

THINKING IT THROUGH

- Is your church already connected to a particular aid or mission agency working among the poor? If so, how could your group support it better? Do they provide a particular set of resources for use with young people?
- Check the web sites of the groups listed in the Taking it Further section. Are there current campaigns you could support and work with?
- Is your church fair-trade? If not, how could your young people encourage it to become so?
- Many aid agencies provide regular updates for youth leaders and ministers. If you are not already on the list, why not contact a group and be put on it?
- Did you know that many agencies have youth workers whose role is to educate and involve young people in these issues? Find out who your regional aid agency youth workers are and invite them to a session, or go to an event they are working on.
- Could your young people create prayers or poems on the theme of poverty for use in the wider church?
- Many churches think about poverty at harvest. How could you draw the issue into other times of the Church's year?

SPARE CHANGE OR ALL CHANGE?

SUMMARY

One theme that has run though this chapter is a question that often leads to a sense of hopelessness or powerlessness: 'What can I do that will actually make a difference?' This is where the rubber hits the road, and all the learning about global injustice needs to make an impact. We can pray about situations of injustice and take action to bring about change. The following section gives plenty of ideas for how we can go about doing this.

The Bible paints a vivid, inspiring image for the future, where one day every tear will be wiped away, there will be no more death or mourning or crying or pain and this old order of things will pass away (Revelation 21.4). This is our hope and vision; and until this day comes whatever we do, no matter how big or small, seemingly effective or not, whatever we do for the least here on earth, we are doing for Christ.

SPARE CHANGE OR ALL CHANGE?

Learning about global injustice can leave us feeling down, wondering if things will ever change. I believe change really is possible; here are some ideas to get you going.

First, we can pray. Praying about these situations, for those in poverty and for world leaders who make decisions that directly affect them, is a real challenge. But it is an essential part of our Christian faith and I believe has an immeasurable effect that can really make a difference. There are all sorts of creative ways of praying. One way, continuing on from the sticker-covered globe (see the Case Studies section) is to encourage the young people to go away from the meeting and find out more about the country their clothes were made in, with a view to writing a prayer for that country. Or they could dedicate themselves to pray for that country for a set period of time. This helps to develop the sense of 'loving our neighbour'.

Secondly, we can act: we can do things to help bring about change. Often these actions will be small and feel insignificant, but they do bring about real change. There are simple things like signing a postcard or writing to your local MP, or the more wacky, like drawing a picture that becomes a part of the world's biggest dress (see Speak's Big Dress campaign; the dress is due to be touring the UK in 2007 – www.speak.org.uk/thebigdress).

Some web sites for youth work resources

www.christian-aid.org/mpower/index.htm
youth.tearfund.org/youth+leader/
www.cafod.org.uk/resources/youth_leaders

Aimed at young people to help them get more information and fired up about campaigning

youth.tearfund.org/
www.pressureworks.org/
www.cafod.org.uk/fasttrack/

More general campaign web sites with in-depth reports, specific campaign actions and ideas for praying

www.speak.org.uk/
www.wdm.org.uk/
www.maketradefair.com
www.christian-aid.org/
www.tearfund.org/
www.cafod.org.uk/

Each of these web sites will list current campaigns and projects in which your group could become practically involved. In addition, for Anglican youth leaders, most Church of England dioceses have links with churches in the poorer parts of the Anglican Communion. These links may also provide opportunities for service, learning and action.

RETHINKING YOUNG PEOPLE AND MISSION

Those who commit themselves to working with young people are not often described as bored. Whether a volunteer leader or a paid youth worker, there is always something more that could be done, someone else to talk to, or another event to prepare for. In the midst of all the activity it can be hard to find the space to step back and think. However, being active and being effective are not necessarily the same thing.

The final section of this book presents four chapters designed to help youth workers and church leaders reflect on their practice, motives and cultural settings. We do not work with young people in a vacuum; both they and we are incredibly influenced by the culture in which we live.

Nicholas Shepherd looks at the influence of tourism on the way we see mission, particularly exploring how the currently popular large-scale, short-term mission events may be shaped and understood by a generation influenced by the experience of tourism.

Not having enough time to achieve everything we want is a frustration shared by all youth leaders, be they volunteers or paid. Having moved from a parish church in an affluent suburb to a ministry in a prison, Helen Dearnley explores how we choose to deploy our limited resources for mission with young people and who should have the first demand on our time.

A first degree in English and an MA in Religious Studies have led Alison Booker to a fascination with the way words hinder or help our task in reaching young people. She explores how language works and whether we need a new language to reach young people today.

Steve Hollinghurst then looks at some of the cultural factors that cause young people to leave the Church. Steve is a full-time researcher into evangelism in postmodern culture, working at Church Army's Sheffield Centre, and a former university chaplain.

Finally, a postscript explores some of the tensions that must continually be addressed by those who work with young people as they seek to keep their mission to young people relevant.

These chapters provide no easy answers for youth leaders. They do, however, help us to understand the setting in which we carry out our mission and to recognize the pressures upon both ourselves and young people.

11 MISSION AS PACKAGE HOLIDAY?
Problems and possibilities in 'mass action mission events'

Nicholas Shepherd

INTRODUCTION

In recent years there has been a swathe of 'events' focused on mission, which have grown out of Christian festivals in the UK. I call these events 'mass action missions' because they share very similar hallmarks: large numbers of young people undertaking large-scale practical/action projects with evening worship or music events. In this chapter I will argue that mass action mission events have much in common with the 'package holiday' and the participants are as much 'tourists' as missionaries. I do not deny that these events do good, blessing both participants and local communities. However, this tourism also has potential downsides which we would do well to heed.

THE ISSUE: The mass action mission – a decade's worth of evangelism

Message 2000 was the first of these 'mass action missions'. Message 2000 was an initiative of local churches in Manchester and (the then) Message to Schools Trust, supported by many Christian agencies including Soul Survivor. This event drew young people to Manchester to undertake social action projects and enjoy a series of evening music events. This would later be replicated in 2003 as Festival Manchester. In parallel to involvement in Festival Manchester, Soul Survivor also generated the idea for, and galvanized participation in, Soul in the City (SITC). SITC brought thousands of young people to London in the summer of 2004, again with a focus on engaging in mission projects. In the summer of 2005, a similar mission was organized in Merseyside – MerseyFest. This event didn't replicate the scale of incoming participants as SITC did, but did function on the same basic model of 'action' projects and worship events.[1] In July 2006, the Diocese of Birmingham's centenary focus on youth (B-cent) was a similar mass action mission event.[2] In addition, the 'success' of SITC has prompted Soul Survivor to establish a new charity, Soul Action, to stimulate 'social action and mission'. The link to SITC is explicit, as their web site reports:

> During the summer of 2004, 11,500 Christian young people joined with 9,000 London churchgoers from 772 of the Capital's churches

for a massive citywide initiative seeing communities and individuals across London on the receiving end of acts of service, love and compassion . . . It sounds crazy but Soul Action is working alongside Soul Survivor and local Durban (South Africa) churches to launch a similar initiative in 2009.[3]

Over the last five years, then, these types of missions have become a near essential component of summer activities for many youth groups. For some young people they will provide the key formative experiences that influence their perceptions and desires for ongoing mission in their locality, lives and future. Unpacking mass action mission (such as SITC) is therefore more than an academic exercise. Mass action missions could form a valuable part of mission in the twenty-first century; they have a lot to offer and a great deal of potential. However, this shouldn't be accepted just because 'the brochure' or promo video tells us so! We need to examine more closely the cultural influences that shape such missions and appreciate both the positive and negative effects these bring, and that is what I intend to do in this chapter. I will begin by outlining how the cultural influence of tourism affects mission and then focus more specifically on how this is observed in the 'mass action missions'. To conclude I will offer some suggestions for how youth workers can respond practically to both the problems and possibilities in 'mission as package holiday'.

> **'These types of missions have become a near essential component of summer activities for many youth groups. For some young people they will provide the key formative experiences that influence their perceptions and desires for ongoing mission in their locality, lives and future.'**

THEORY: Mission, culture and tourism

Mission is a complex business. The task of communicating the gospel, seeking to fulfil and enact the Good News, is not a matter of following simple patterns or methods. I like the way that David Bosch, the late South African missiologist, summarizes the reality of mission. He says,

> Our missionary practice is not performed in unbroken continuity with the biblical witness; it is an altogether ambivalent enterprise executed in the context of tension between divine providence and human confusion.[4]

Mission requires creativity and imagination, boldness and determination, sensitivity and insight. Yet no matter how hard we pray, plan and work, we will never fully know what we're doing or achieving! What is of paramount importance, though, is to try to connect our 'missions' with God's agenda and activity in mission: what is known as Missio Dei. I am sure that those who plan and participate in 'mass action missions' are trying to do just this. I am also sure that God by his Spirit uses such events to bless and transform lives. So what's the problem?

The problem is that when we undertake mission, or any church-related activity, our culture shapes both our theology and actions. This influence is not always noticeable, and it is often only years later that biases are identified and the repercussions recognized. Bosch, in his book *Transforming Mission*, discusses this phenomenon when he describes 'paradigms' in mission. A strong example of a paradigm is the way in which mission and colonialism related in nineteenth- and early twentieth-century mission. Bosch argues (and others agree) that the cultural force of colonialism was a profound influence on motivation and methods for mission.[5] To this end, mission and colonialism were often coterminous projects, with missionaries serving as cultural evangelists for 'the Empire' as well as carriers of the gospel.[6] This meant that the infrastructure for mission was dependent on that established for colonialism and the spread of mission positively supported the expansion of empire. This cultural bias is well recognized in writing on mission.[7] However, what is not so clear

> 'When we undertake mission, or any church-related activity, our culture shapes both our theology and actions.'

are the ways in which we may be developing mission with biases of our own. What could be a critical cultural influence on our approach to mission? I suggest that a strong candidate is tourism.

Tourism affects our approach to mission in two principal ways. First, it is a deeply influential cultural motif that shapes the way we view the world and live in it. Second, the tourist industry that serves and sustains the culture of tourism has certain organizing principles and practices. These two factors are clearly seen in the operation of events such as SITC, as I will outline in the next two sections.

The tourist-missionary

Tourism is intricately connected to leisure. The way in which we divide our time into work and leisure, or school and holiday, is a key feature of modern life. Tourism is a use of leisure time and the purpose of travel is leisure. Personal motivations guide the selection of when and where to travel and what activities to engage in (package holidays, mountain trekking, working holidays) but all tourists are leisured travellers and vice versa.[8] Tourists leave their ordinary world and life behind and reside for a time in an 'extra-ordinary' place/culture; subsequently returning to the life they left behind.[9] By this definition, the young person who goes on a 'mass action mission' event is thus a tourist.[10] This in itself is not a problem; it is an aspect of our culture that we have adopted and shaped.

> **'Tourists leave their ordinary world and life behind and reside for a time in an "extra-ordinary" place/culture; subsequently returning to the life they left behind. By this definition, the young person who goes on a "mass action mission" event is thus a tourist.'**

However, the strength of a tourist experience is in its difference to normal life. The new country, exciting pursuit, exotic location or poolside romance provide experiences and memories that act as an enhancement to normal life and for some as an antidote to its stresses. As a result, people act differently on holiday. We can be more carefree and spontaneous; we can hide away or escape. The same is true for the missionary-tourist. This is not our week-in, week-out environment. We can be a little bolder about our faith; we can try things we never thought we'd be capable of – and be surprised and pleased at ourselves. This could of course be of real benefit for young people, enabling them to understand more about who they are and exploring their faith.

However, there is a potential downside. The experience becomes the main benefit of the trip and the tourist then seeks a new experience to match or better it next year. In addition, connecting the experience of being away to everyday life can be quite difficult. The excitement and feeling of involvement in mission can ebb away, leaving the thought of going on next year's event as the only interest in 'mission'. This was emphasized to me by one young man, wearing a SITC T-shirt, whom I saw at Paddington station the day after SITC ended. I introduced myself and said that I had been involved in the mission. He was very positive about his week in North London, so I asked him what he was most looking forward to when he went home. His reply was, 'I can't wait for Liverpool.'

Is the tourist-missionary then something we should encourage or dissuade? Those who organize short-term mission trips have long faced the challenges of balancing a young person getting 'an experience' from a mission trip and the tangible input they bring to an ongoing mission. The influence of tourism on our psyche means that we will always struggle to be otherwise on short trips to new places. However, 'mass action mission' events actually lean towards providing *only* a touristic experience. This is due to their 'mass nature', as I will now explain.

> **'Is the tourist-missionary then something we should encourage or dissuade?'**

NEED TO KNOW: Managing mission as tourism – putting the package in its place

Missionaries who spend a longer time period in a place can become even more integrated into the local community. Small groups of travellers can be relatively easily absorbed into a host culture, and as such get a fairly accurate glimpse of the life and customs of the people they are staying with. However, a key lesson from studies on tourism is that this ability is severely hampered when the numbers go up and the time in the location decreases. Such mass tourism has particular problems and provokes some very harsh critiques on the damage it does to host cultures.[11] The mechanism that is used to manage the difficulties is the 'package holiday'.

The tourist is firstly sold a destination through a brochure. This lets them know a little about where they are going, but also presents a particular image of what they will find and experience there. Accommodation provided for tourists is with other tourists in resorts that are often separated off from local towns. However, to get the flavour of the locality, excursions are put on so that tourists may experience the local culture, cuisine and sights. In addition, the resorts themselves are designed to represent facets of the local situation but provide the standards and facilities that the tourists are used to in their home culture.

In SITC the first contact most delegates had with the mission was the brochure and the promo video. This sold London as a destination for mission and SITC as an exciting event to be involved in. On arrival in London, the young people were accommodated in tent cities, temporary resorts designed to replicate the teaching and worship of a Soul Survivor festival.[12] The excursions during the day were to the 'mission' projects staged for the event itself.[13] This effectively managed the large numbers involved as well as any package holiday could. Partner church projects were also able to allocate smaller teams.[14]

Only two hours a day at most were spent in the projects and most churches therefore used the delegates for 'self-contained' projects specifically prepared in advance for SITC. From the point of view of the delegate this was largely accepted as being involved in the churches' ongoing mission. However, some delegates complained of a lack of contact with local young people – this staging of mission left them disappointed. In addition, some partner churches felt disappointed that local people could not follow up contacts or that delegates either pushed conversation on faith too far or too little. Overall, there was a feeling of a lack of time to engage in activities that were more meaningful.[15]

This is unsurprising. Authentic mission needs authentic cultural contact and exchange between the 'gospel' community and the local community.[16] As the Shaftesbury Society report on SITC points out,[17] package mission, in order to cope with the large numbers involved, provides a limited experience of mission because it is impossible to do otherwise. However, tourism studies explain this through the insight that it is not possible to integrate such numbers of visitors in such a short timescale into a dynamic cultural exchange.

> 'Authentic mission needs authentic cultural contact and exchange between the "gospel" community and the local community.'

Is the package mission then something we should encourage or deter? Replication of these types of events will replicate only the successes and frustrations associated with the package holiday form of tourism (of which I have only mentioned a fraction). What we should seek to do, then, is put the package in its place! There are other ways of organizing tourism and so there are other ways of organizing mission, even in a tourist paradigm.

CASE STUDY: Motivating mission through tourism – regenerating involvement and reigniting passion

So far I have been fairly harsh in my critique of 'mass action missions' and we do need to heed the warnings offered by tourism studies on the cultural effects on hosts and the limited authenticity of package holidays. However, I do not wish to suggest that the influences of tourism, or even the package project missions, are inherently 'bad'. To this end I wish to highlight two ways that they could be very beneficial. These two principles are seen within understandings of tourism. Just as tourism can be a way of regenerating a local economy, a

> 'Just as tourism can be a way of regenerating a local economy, a "mass action mission" can kick-start a local "mission" economy.'

'mass action mission' can kick-start a local 'mission' economy. Just as a holiday can provoke a deeper interest in a cultural or sporting pursuit and/or a geographical location, participating in a 'mass action mission' can ignite a passion for a particular city or people group, or for an ongoing involvement in social action.

SITC did bring London churches together. It did provide a focal point for mission and did stimulate fresh networks and relationships which, along with some physical regeneration projects, have left a 'legacy'. In the summer of 2005, several churches and organizations carried on joint working in order to put on SITC activities similar to those that ran in 2004, but driven through the input of local people. Some of the delegates who worked on projects in 2004 came back for the summer of 2005. This is encouraging and positive, but to develop this potential requires active input from young people and youth workers that goes beyond simply doing the package and going home. To this end I wish to conclude this chapter by offering three tips to maximize the potential of the tourist-missionary!

THINKING IT THROUGH: How to be a good (mission) tour rep or (gospel) travel agent!

How can we encourage young people to reflect both pre and post event?

We shouldn't accept uncritically the brochure pitch that participation in a 'mass action mission' is inevitably a positive and inspiring time for our young people. Likewise, we shouldn't be surprised if our young people gain a vision and insight for mission beyond what we expected or thought possible. We need to approach such events as youth workers – working with our young people to help them get the most out of the mission, rather than simply handing them over to get caught up in the event's organization and processes without reflection. We

> 'We should actively help young people to think through the aims and fruit of their efforts and the influence of their experiences.'

should actively help young people to think through the aims and fruit of their efforts and the influence of their experiences. This doesn't have to be 'heavy'; it could be a pre-event prayer meeting and a post-event social evening looking at photos and telling stories. However we do it, we need to help young people prepare for and unpack their package mission.

How can we encourage young people to form longer-term connections and commitments?

Our use of such package events should be matched by a determination to foster a longer-term connection to a mission project or location. Going to the same place year after year with the same young people can both help our appreciation of what is required in mission and also allow young people to build on their experiences and learning. This could be a connection made initially through a mass action mission or a youth group's contribution to support an existing church missionary link.

How can we encourage young people to have a variety of experiences?

We should encourage young people to gain a variety of 'mission' experiences – working in a local shelter or children's club, taking a six-month gap project, planning a summer scheme for a local estate. Rather than taking a package, perhaps you might consider becoming a more independent traveller in organizing mission trips. This increases the roles that young people themselves can undertake in preparing, planning, running and reflecting on a mission trip.

MISSION AS PACKAGE HOLIDAY?

SUMMARY

Finally, even with all the reservations I have about package mission, if we go we do need to encourage enjoyment. Mission isn't, and shouldn't be, always enjoyable, but an enjoyable mission experience is a good start and a great memory. 'Mass action mission' events can be exhilarating and fun. Groups can bond and individuals can grow. If our young people enjoy being involved in social action projects, and other forms of mission, then we stand more chance of them involving themselves in similar work in the future.

In this chapter I have examined how 'mass action missions', such as Soul in the City, are influenced by the cultural phenomenon of tourism and are organized on the principles of the package holiday. Mission is always influenced by our culture and I have unpacked two of the potential problems that arise from the influence of tourism. The first is the ways in which individuals participating in 'mass action missions' are similar to tourists – a role that confuses purpose and participation. The second is the application of the motif of the package holiday to the organization and implementation of 'mass action mission'. This causes difficulties from a missiological viewpoint in effective contact and also in how large numbers can be effectively managed.

I finished with two positive points on how 'mass action mission' could help regenerate mission or reignite a passion for mission and three suggestions for how we can encourage young people to get the most from participating in 'mass action missions'.

MISSION AS PACKAGE HOLIDAY?

If you are interested in reading more on how tourism and the package holiday influence 'mass action mission' events, I expound on the themes of this chapter in slightly more detail in a paper, 'Soul in the City – Mission as Package Holiday', published in the journal *Anvil* (Vol. 22, No. 4). The projects I have mentioned all have a web site and the Soul Action web page has information on the principles they see as being the driving force behind their work, as well as heaps of practical information. If you are considering taking your group off somewhere independently, then most of the mission agencies (CMS, BMS, Tearfund etc.) can offer you support, as well as organized gap year projects. Local churches are also forming their own direct mission links to places overseas.

12 CHURCH HALL vs LYCHGATE: Which young people should we focus our mission efforts on?

Helen Dearnley

INTRODUCTION – Restricted resources mean tough choices

> Money's too tight to mention,
> The stereotype is true.
> The church roof it is leaking,
> And there is woodworm in the pew,
> a toilet is now needed
> and the hymn books are not new!
>
> Time's too tight to mention,
> The people always say
> Asked to do so many things
> They turn and look away
> When volunteers are needed
> We'll try another day!

Poetry may never have been my strongest point but the issues raised here in fun infect the Church at the most serious of levels. We, the Church, have limited resources in both time and money. There simply isn't enough of either to do everything we would wish. We have to make hard choices. One of those choices is how we meet the need for mission and evangelism amongst young people. The decisions don't end there. Once we have scraped together some time and money, who do we invest it in? What focus will bring us the greatest reward or benefit? Who do we work with?

THE ISSUE: Time the first frontier

Jesus told the parable of the Good Samaritan to illustrate the need to take time to love the unlovable, no matter what the purpose of your journey. As you reflect on that story, who do you think you are? Most of us I am sure would like to think that our behaviour mirrors that of the title character. If we saw someone lying injured in the road, of course we would stop to help, but life is often more subtle than that. When a crisis occurs it is easy to drop everything we are doing and help. However, in the routine of daily life we are often complacent and fail to see the myriad of needs on our doorstep.

If a crisis is only understood as a life-changing event or emergency which breaks the pattern of daily life, then we can become immune to the daily trials of everyday life. Faces we see every day may mask a crisis but in our complacency or simple busyness with our own lives we fail to interact at any deeper than surface level with those around us. We ask 'How are you?' but only ever hear 'Fine' in response – the unspoken feelings go unnoticed.

In my first post I often only had time for a cursory 'Hello, are you all right, lads?' to the young men drinking cans and smoking at the lychgate.[1] I rarely even waited for a reply as I raced past to lead the church youth club. The model that the Sunday routine foisted upon me as I rushed from service to service and on to the youth group mirrored more the image of the Priest and Levite than it did the Good Samaritan.

> **'In my first post I often only had time for a cursory "Hello, are you all right, lads?" to the young men drinking cans and smoking at the lychgate. I rarely even waited for a reply as I raced past to lead the church youth club.'**

Looking back on my time in that first parish it is now possible to reflect on my motivation, whereas at the time I became absorbed in activity to the exclusion of calculated thought. Now it seems to me that pressure was exerted on me both internally and externally. I felt I 'ought' to get to know these lads, indeed, that I had a spiritual duty to do so, but that sense of spiritual duty arguably came from how other people saw me as much as the operation of my own conscience. Far from being intentional, hindsight has enabled me to realize that my compassion towards those lads was effectively lip service, born in part out of the positive affirmation of others at my actions. The action of simply saying 'Hello' was more than many others even attempted. In that action I, in some small way, salved their conscience. There was no challenge or expectation for either myself or anyone else to do any more. Each week I walked on by to keep the status quo, to fulfil what was desired and expected of me by parents from the church community, concerned that their own children had appropriate Christian teaching.

If I could turn the clock back would I have done anything differently? With the confidence I now have, I hope I would stand up against the prevailing culture and spend more time getting to know the lads at the lychgate. This would have to be at the expense of some other laudable parish business, and no doubt would bring pressure from the church community. No-one would say investing time at the lychgate was time badly spent; conflict would occur, however, if other work was curtailed in order to provide the space to build such relationships. The challenging issue would have to be raised of the needs of the lychgate kids as opposed to the needs of the kids who regularly attended the youth group in the church hall. What was needed was not simply a change of my own actions but a cultural shift within the wider church community.

Such a cultural shift can occur only if the church community faces up to the realities of each group, recognizing the emotional, physical and spiritual investment involved. As youth leaders we will need to recognize our own motivation, our need to be needed, and see that against our desire to be popular within our own community. These considerations are mirrored at a corporate level by the church community, who are equally concerned with how they are perceived by the society they serve.

'As youth leaders we will need to recognize our own motivation, our need to be needed, and see that against our desire to be popular within our own community. These considerations are mirrored at a corporate level by the church community, who are equally concerned with how they are perceived by the society they serve.'

Arguably the church hall kids would be the easiest for most of us to work with, as we are often deepening faith in those who have already begun that journey. In many cases their backgrounds are similar to our own; they have a working knowledge of 'church' and what 'church' means and indeed expects of them. Good and appropriate resource materials are readily available to guide our programme planning. Our teaching is often, although not always, supported and encouraged by their home environment. The questions they ask us are often challenging and informed. Their behaviour may fit more easily our expectations and desires of a 'good group'. Here we can find ourselves not challenging the status quo but merely fulfilling the expectations of the church community.

There is an assumption that the lychgate kids provide a greater challenge. Their only knowledge of church may be a telling off for the cans and bottles they leave in their wake. Yet they may be an open book, a field ready to be harvested, a disaffected group ready to be loved. Often their background differs greatly from our own; they may never have set foot in a church and wouldn't necessarily know what to do if they did. There are very few appropriate resources available for youth workers ministering to such a group. Any teaching given would be in isolation from the rest of their circle of influence. Their questioning may be crude and blunt, providing a sense that any formal teaching methods appear to be unrealistic or at best a long way off. Their conduct and attitude may be intimidating.

We have to choose: do we invest our limited resources with the church hall kids who have perhaps already begun a journey of discipleship, or do we invest in the lychgate kids who may never have heard the word 'disciple'?

> 'We have to choose: do we invest our limited resources with the church hall kids who have perhaps already begun a journey of discipleship, or do we invest in the lychgate kids who may never have heard the word "disciple"?'

With whom do we invest our precious time and energy?

THEORY/BACKGROUND TO THE ISSUE: Inside out

I believe that our mission and evangelism is shaped by three motivational factors, which can be summarized as Internal, External and Theological. This section tackles Internal and Theological motivation; External motivation is explored later under 'Need to know'.

Internal motivation

Internal motivation includes the powerful emotions of 'trust' and 'fear'. Personality and gifting will cause each youth worker to react in a unique way. One person's dream is for another a living nightmare. We need to recognize and accept which group our skills and gifting naturally equip us to engage with. Taking an example from my current ministry, the environment of a prison would disable some people from exercising an effective ministry, as they become crippled by the claustrophobic nature of the building. In contrast, others, myself included, feel alive and free in such an institution, despite its obvious confines.

Which kind of young people we find easier to trust will depend upon our ability to relate to the groups. The ability to trust will be born out of our history and experiences, a complex web of family background, personality, socialization and psychology.

Acts 10 brings sharply into focus how a lack of knowledge and received prejudice between two groups can cause fear. Examples of this can be seen throughout history, often resulting in a ghetto mentality that raises the potential for violence, ethnic cleansing or genocide. While recognizing that one group may instil fear in us, for whatever reason, be it their difference or our perceived inadequacy, we are called to act not out of fear but out of love. As Peter recognized that the gift of the Holy Spirit was poured out on Jew and Gentile alike, so we must not forget to look for God at work in the group we find most difficult and be willing to follow God to them.

> **'As Peter recognized that the gift of the Holy Spirit was poured out on Jew and Gentile alike, so we must not forget to look for God at work in the group we find most difficult and be willing to follow God to them.'**

Theological motivation

Theological motivation is when we are moved to act in a particular way because of our understanding of God. Such understanding is gained from our engagement with Scripture, church tradition, reason and personal experience. Such engagement forms us as Christians and so motivates our actions.

When Christ sent out the 70 (Luke 10) he asked them to go and find people who shared in their peace. Our call mirrors theirs. When we engage with either group, lychgate or church hall, we need to discern who the individuals of peace are: individuals willing to listen and engage with the Christian message. People of peace could be found within either group. The only way for us to discover where people of peace are is for us to go to them and ask! If they are willing to listen, our ministry will be heard. If they are not, either another approach must be sought or, as in verses 10 and 11, we need to shake the dust off our feet (metaphorically!) and move on, reinvesting ourselves elsewhere. There is a twofold challenge involved here: the first is in going to each group regardless of our personal prejudices. The second acknowledges our own frailties and feelings of failure when we are called to walk away.

Throughout Church history God's bias to the poor has often been a focus for people's attention. From almsgiving to the Make Poverty History campaign, Christian communities have been encouraged to recognize how their lifestyle differs from that of their brothers and sisters and to act in order to bring about justice for the poor. This raises the question, 'Who is poor?' Our current usage of the word 'poor' usually describes individuals who are without material wealth. This is in contrast to a theological understanding. The Scriptures enable us to understand the concept of poverty in a wider context that includes the materially poor (Isaiah 61.1, GNB) but also those who are oppressed (NRSV and CEV) or meek (KJV). Jesus further expands our understanding of

> ' "Who is poor?" Our current usage of the word "poor" usually describes individuals who are without material wealth. This is in contrast to a theological understanding.'

poverty in his Sermon on the Mount, in which we are taught 'Blessed are the poor in spirit, for theirs is the kingdom of heaven . . . Blessed are the meek, for they will inherit the earth . . . Blessed are those who are persecuted for righteousness' sake, for theirs is the kingdom of heaven' (Matthew 5.3,5, 10). Poverty then is not simply understood as a lack of material wealth; it also incorporates a lack of spiritual nourishment.

Being called to the poor raises complex questions. Who is the poorer? The inner city child whose worn-out trousers are lovingly patched by his mother, or the suburban child who sees her parents only on Sunday evening when the allowance cheque is given?

NEED TO KNOW: Hard pressed on every side

External motivation is understood to include any pressures placed upon us by outside agencies. These include the following.

Pressures on time

There are simply not enough hours in the day to achieve all we would wish. We are therefore forced to make decisions about where we invest our time. Further limitations may be placed on the paid youth worker by the length of contract available. The shorter the contract the more realistic the youth worker must be as to what can be achieved. It may be that although a particular youth worker has all the necessary gifting to develop a new ministry with those at the lychgate, the time available to them simply will not allow it, and to begin a new ministry without long-term support for such young people would be inappropriate.

> 'There are simply not enough hours in the day to achieve all we would wish. We are therefore forced to make decisions about where we invest our time.'

Varied voices

These could also be called external pressure groups! Groups who exercise pressure on us about our priorities often include the church council or the parents of 'church hall' kids who feel that the church's first duty is to 'its own'. Although they do not negate the ministry to 'lychgate' kids, in their opinion it should be in addition to, rather than instead of, provision for the 'church hall' kids. Further pressure is exerted when such groups do not want the 'lychgate' kids to mix with the 'church hall' kids, because they are the 'wrong sort'. If unchecked, these external pressure groups further increase the divide between the 'church hall' kids and those at the 'lychgate'.

Expectations placed on paid workers

A paid youth worker may have been employed (and funding raised) for a specific project, which may be either to nurture children within the church or to reach out to 'lychgate' kids. Tensions obviously occur when the worker deviates from their specific brief into a wider ministry.

If the funding is not specific the will of the employer may be a deciding factor as to which group the worker may minister to.

CASE STUDY: All that glitters isn't gold

Currently I am the coordinating chaplain of a local prison in which staff are involved, amongst other duties, in challenging the lifestyles of young people that may result in crime and custodial sentencing. Prison officers enable youngsters who have begun to be involved in criminal activities to spend time with staff and prisoners to see for themselves what life inside is really like. The confident and cocky teenagers that arrive leave in a more sober and reflective mood after they have experienced the cells and spoken to some of the lads who are serving time.

When their short time with us is over, these youngsters have a choice to make: either to go back to their old routines and risk experiencing prison for real, or to change their actions and begin a new life away from the vices of the past.

Although in receipt of many messages of thanks, the prison staff have no idea about the effect of their work with the young people who enter the prison on these 'taster' visits. There is no way of determining which of the youngsters would have entered prison without the experience. All we are sure of is that their lives were heading in a bad direction.

This provides a challenge to our thinking particularly in the area of 'fruit', by which I mean the measurable effectiveness of a particular ministry. There is strong biblical foundation for validating our ministry by the 'fruit' that it bears. Jesus' words regarding leaders are clear: 'You will know them by their fruits . . . every good tree bears good fruit, but the bad tree bears bad fruit . . . Thus you will know them by their fruits' (Matthew 7.16-20). However, as with the case study, the work that we undertake with young people doesn't always have an obvious fruit that can be used to assess whether our actions are successful or not.

Rarely do we see the fruits of our labour with young people, the harvest often being brought in years later. This creates an internal dilemma. How can we justify our ministry among young people if we cannot prove its effectiveness? For some the solution is found by narrowing expectations – justification for effective youth ministry becomes merely the number of individuals converted, or attendance figures at a particular event, to the exclusion of wider missionary activities. This 'tunnel vision' affirms the youth worker and is often the marker used when resources are allocated. However, this need for numbers can become a 'false fruit', a bad apple, as it can restrict God's mission too narrowly in our minds.

> **'Rarely do we see the fruits of our labour with young people, the harvest often being brought in years later.'**

Further, when we are forced to choose (in the hypothetical lychgate vs church hall dilemma) where to invest our resources, we must be prepared to live with the 'might have been'. In living with the consequences of our actions we must accept that our care cannot extend to all and our choices necessarily act positively with one group and negatively with another. Metaphorically we are forced to walk by on the other side, leaving some young people alone simply because we cannot be in two places at once!

There are no easy answers but a time for honest self-analysis is required. Are we motivated by our own need to prove our worth to others? Are we motivated by the perceived difficulty of the task ahead? Are we acting out of an 'ought to' or 'should do' mentality? Are we reacting out of fear and intimidation – from the church council?! Whom are we trying to please? Whose approval do we seek? Are we aware of our own gifting and ability? It is all too easy to think that the lychgate kids are the ones we should help, but in reality there is no clear-cut solution. Both groups are loved by God and deserve our resources; which group gains the investment will depend upon the gifting and calling of those who minister in a particular area.

When ministering, a decision needs to be made about what we are trying to achieve, and here again there is no quantifiable outcome. It may be possible to bring half the church hall kids to a point of recognition and ownership of faith for themselves, but is that better or worse than enabling half the lychgate kids to glimpse the saving character of Christ? No easy answers, no easy solution. We will never know the full consequences for those who do not receive the investment, whichever group that may be.

Those young people who visit the prison have their eyes opened to a world they do not want to be part of, a world of isolation and loneliness, a world that by their actions they can choose to enter or leave behind. The responsibility we hold as we engage in mission and evangelism is to open the eyes of those we meet to a world of love, hope, life and salvation beyond their wildest dreams.

Secular missionaries?
Mission may be understood as bringing to humanity the values of the kingdom. Those values arguably include bringing the good news to the poor and freeing prisoners from the bonds of sin (see Isaiah 61 and Luke 4). These values can be seen at work in organizations such as those who seek to achieve fair trade, human rights and access to medical care. When this work is done under the banner of Cafod, Christian Aid or Tear Fund it fits easily with our understanding of mission. Could the work of secular charities be understood in the same way? Similarly, each chapter of this book shows mission under an overtly Christian umbrella. Is it possible to argue that the work undertaken by, for example, the prison staff is indeed part of God's mission? The prophet Nehemiah shows us an example of a 'secular' king, Artaxerxes, who advances the kingdom by enabling the rebuilding of Jerusalem's walls through his support of Nehemiah. In the same way the

'secular' prison staff through their actions enable 'metanoia'[2] in the lives of the young people that visit the prison as they turn away from parts of their destructive lifestyle.

At the broadest level this raises further questions. How can the Church, charged with the duty and joy of evangelism, engage with the 'secular' agents of God's mission? More narrowly, it asks each of us individually where and with whom we are prepared to engage in the mission of God. Will we do our mission within the safety of the church or will we engage in the mission of bringing wholeness to a broken world with those outside the church walls?

> **'Will we do our mission within the safety of the church or will we engage in the mission of bringing wholeness to a broken world with those outside the church walls?'**

THINKING IT THROUGH: Who's in control?

- Do the young people have a voice in where your resources go? Do you listen to the church hall kid or the kid at the lychgate? Whose opinion do you value? Which group do you find easier to talk to? Who shapes what you think about each group? Which group do you most enjoy being with?
- What are we trying to achieve: what are the effects of engaging with the church hall kids? What are the effects of engaging with the lychgate kids?
- Which external voice has the stronger influence on us? Parents? Church leaders?
- Who can you share these issues with? How do you handle the frustration of our limited resources?

CHURCH HALL vs. LYCHGATE

SUMMARY

This chapter raises issues for the youth worker and the church alike. It forces us to question our ministry at its very core. We are challenged to be vulnerable and to be prepared to change how and where we spend our time.

In raising the issues about the two groups we must always be aware of where the power lies and of Christ's imperative to speak for those without a voice. We must be confident enough in ourselves to argue where the resources need to be invested, rather than simply follow the loudest voices that cry for our time and energy.

We must recognize that we are motivated in three ways in our mission and evangelism among young people:

> Internally
> Externally
> Theologically.

We are left with difficult questions about ourselves and about mission itself. Who has the greater need? Are we able to minister to either group? What would the effect of our ministry be upon our own community? There are no easy answers for us, but these are questions we must prayerfully face.

CHURCH HALL vs. LYCHGATE

William Noblett, *Prayers for People in Prison*, Oxford University Press, 1998.

Robin Greenwood, *Transforming Church*, SPCK, 2002.

David J. Bosch, *Transforming Mission*, Orbis Books, 1991.

TAKING IT FURTHER

13 SPEAKING IN TONGUES? Is our language stopping us communicating with young people?

Alison Booker

INTRODUCTION: It's all Greek to me!

When missionaries are sent abroad their initial training often includes an orientation course, and particularly the chance to learn the language they are going to need to master in order to communicate the gospel where they are sent. I often think that youth workers ought to be allowed the same amount of time, not to learn Spanish, French or Swahili, but to learn Years 7, 8, 9, 10 and 11, not to mention College speak, University speak and 20s speak, in all their various dialects! It is perhaps a very strange thing to say, but language, like the air we breathe, is not something we think about very often, yet it is a vital part of the world in which we live.

I am passionate about language: not just the way we speak but the kind of language that we use. I believe that it can either help or hinder our missionary efforts more than almost any other single factor and because of this it deserves more attention than we usually give it!

THE ISSUE: Learning a new language

Current British society seems to have lost the significant place that was once held by traditional religious phrases. Of course, society also now moves on so quickly that we are constantly dealing, in a way that we haven't before, with a new generation and new ways of seeing the world. Back in 1991 Douglas Coupland wrote a book called *Generation X*, which encapsulated a whole generation of young people. The book included definitions of 'new' words, one of which was 'Me-ism – a search by an individual in the absence of training in traditional religious tenets to formulate a personally tailored religion by himself.'[1] There is a sense in which Coupland is saying that Generation X is searching for the meaning it has lost.

However, today's young adults, sometimes described as Generation Y, seem to have very different properties! The recent book *Making Sense of Generation Y* begins to explore this new generation (those aged 15–25) and their worldview. The researchers found that 'A shared, traditional religious language to describe God was simply absent'[2] amongst the young people questioned. Like Generation X, Generation Y doesn't seem to relate to traditional 'religious' language, but it appears that Generation Y has also moved further away from feeling any 'need' for religion or its language at all.[3]

The question for youth workers is whether this matters or not. It is my belief that if it doesn't matter to us then it should! Language is the way in which we communicate most of what we think, feel and believe. If we allow the void of language concerning Christian truth to continue, we could find ourselves unable to engage in any kind of mission at all. It would be as though we were missionaries parachuted into the middle of Africa with no language skills and faced with a people who spoke only Kikuyu. Without shared words, how can we communicate?

> **'Language is the way in which we communicate most of what we think, feel and believe. If we allow the void of language concerning Christian truth to continue, we could find ourselves unable to engage in any kind of mission at all.'**

Alongside that challenge there is another question about our own language of faith. Do we who work with young people use our Christian language without fully understanding what we mean by it? If we do, then we shall find it more difficult to create a new language that shares our faith with the young people of this generation because we only know the words; we don't fully understand their meaning or the complexity of ideas that lie behind the word. Christians easily use words like redemption, salvation, mission, evangelism, born-again and other such phrases, but if a young person on the street could heard our 'church speak', would they understand it? If they asked us to

> **'Unless we understand our faith and its language fully we cannot begin to translate it into a useful mission language.'**

explain, could we? Unless we understand our faith and its language fully we cannot begin to translate it into a useful mission language.

Creating a mission language is vital in my opinion, but even after we have understood the words we already use there is more to do before we can begin to think about what we might say in a new mission language. It is important to understand how language works, as well as why it is so important.

How does language work?

There are some who would argue that language is one of the characteristics of what it is to be human. Language experts such as Terry Eagleton (Professor of Cultural Theory at Manchester University) would say that 'only where there is language is there "world", in the distinctively human sense'.[4] It might seem a bit extreme but what is being said is that language is really the glue which binds human society together.

Language has two functions which are extremely important when we are thinking about the Church and its mission. The first is that language provides a way for individuals to express themselves; speech is an act of identity. To some extent, each person has a language that is essentially their own, formed as a result of their particular experiences. A rather simple example of this is the 'family' words that are gained, often by the mispronunciation or imagination of a small child, but are not easily understood outside that family. For example, in our household we don't take pistachio nuts out of their shells, we 'hatch' them!

Secondly, of course, in balance with that individual expression, language is very much communal, an expression of community. The linguistics expert Volosinov says that language is 'a two-sided act'.[5] The communal aspect of language can either be the glue in a social group providing social solidarity and a sense of belonging, or else it can be like the fence which stops anyone new from joining. It keeps the distance between those who use it and those who don't. Specialist communities develop their own language. For example, 'computer speak' is a constant mystery to me. Often when I hear it I think I know nothing about computers and should stay away from them! It is a really good picture of how language itself can work and why it is so important in our mission and evangelism to think about our words and how they work. Otherwise we shall prevent people from joining us because they cannot understand or connect to our language.

Who creates language and meaning?

It seems like a very strange question, especially if you have never spent time thinking about the words you use every day and where they come from. However, if we look at language and its meaning being created by a community, then in the age of television much of our language has been helped into existence by the media, particularly advertising. For example, for those of a certain age the question 'Are you with us?' will often elicit the response 'No, I'm with the Woolwich'. Likewise, 'Beans means . . . ?' can be finished with 'Heinz', and in the late 1990s there was a television advert where the person answering the phone would say 'Whaaaaatsuuuup', which quickly

> **'In the age of television much of our language has been helped into existence by the media, particularly advertising.'**

became a standard greeting among young people, as easily understood to them as 'Hello'. Although it is possible that this phrase was in existence before the advert, it was not part of 'mainstream' language in the way that it was after the advert was shown.

Does this mean that the media create our language? I don't think so; they certainly suggest and influence it but a given community must use it in order for it to become common language, at least within that group. If someone had said 'Whaaaaatsuuuup' and nobody had responded, it would never have become part of 'everyday' language for 'mainstream' teenagers. However, if a community begins to pick up and use a word then it becomes part of the shared language understood by those in that community.

Why do communities create language?

Language is created when what already exists proves that it is not up to the job required! As with most 'inventions', when a job needs to be done then a way is found to do it. Presumably the invention of the wheel was driven by the need to move something; the light bulb because people wanted to work even after dark rather than continue the tradition of working with the natural light. At the points where a need is felt then a creative process begins; language is no different.

One practical example of this might be the change in a couple when they are first handed their newborn child. It is a very significant moment for most people; many respond emotionally, some are completely overwhelmed and can even faint! It seems strange how so many different people can share a set of common responses but the 'proof' of the commonality of this is a general concern by the medical staff that new parents should be sitting down when holding their newborn child, as my husband and I experienced with all three of ours! Suddenly, these two people who have always called each other by their first names (or perhaps a nickname if, unlike me, they are very soppy) begin to refer to each other as Mummy and Daddy. The awesome nature of their changing role is reflected in their language; using the words is somehow part of marking the change.

THEORY/BACKGROUND TO THE ISSUE: Theology? What theology?

Theology itself literally means 'words about God', so having understood a little about how language is formed it is important to look at what theology is necessary in order to form a language for Christian mission. Personally, my first foundation stone is always the Trinity; I believe it is the doctrine of the Trinity which makes our language distinctively Christian. As Alan Torrance once said, 'at the heart of the Christian faith there's a Trinitarian dynamic at work. Without it we may as well go home!'[6] It is this idea of God as Trinity, revealing love to the world, that leads people such as David Bosch to say that our entire mission and evangelism is 'a response to what God has already put into effect'.[7]

Mission language . . . identify yourself!

This book has begun to look at what mission means from a variety of angles and the key elements of a 'mission language' will pick up those themes once again. When we are considering how we communicate with young people (or indeed anyone), I think that there are four key elements to the language we use. Mission language is . . .

Communal

It is a language based in community. That isn't surprising if we consider that a mission language is formed from our understanding of God as Trinity, the perfect community. In addition, of course, any mission language takes account of the final aim of evangelism which seeks, as Lynch puts it, to 'bring us into community',[8] which means creating a community of people in relationship with each other and with God. If our mission language is not shared then it really does not work. Only a sense of community and shared language can begin to communicate a faith based on relationship, the relationship of God with humanity and humanity with each other.

'If our mission language is not shared then it really does not work. Only a sense of community and shared language can begin to communicate a faith based on relationship, the relationship of God with humanity and humanity with each other.'

A bridge

Sometimes words are described as 'a bridge thrown down'.[9] If we want to reach others we too must find the words that make a bridge, a bridge that allows them to meet God and to meet God's people. The problem with this, of course, is that we are trying to speak 'truth' and at the same time describe God, who is, by the very nature of being God, indescribable!

Distinct

Many language experts have said that there is no single common language shared equally by everyone; what happens more often is that although 'English' is the common shared language there will be regional variations across the UK, and within those regions communities may have adapted language further. This should mean that a language for Christian mission will be different from anything else because it is influenced by Christian beliefs and assumptions. A mission language can only be distinct if it is Christian, for it must take account of words such as 'Trinity', which has a distinctive Christian meaning of one God, three persons. The challenge is to create a distinctive language that can still be understood by those outside.

Iconic

That is a language that points to a reality bigger than itself and beyond expression. The clearest example of 'iconic' is probably objects we call symbols which begin to open a clear reality, layered with meaning, layer upon layer gathered over time. This kind of language is often used in Christian worship or prayer, where phrases are understood by the Christian community and clearly point them to the reality beyond themselves that is God. For example the phrase 'we are one body because we all share in one bread' carries with it the significance of sharing physical bread together, but also the symbolism of the church community being the 'body of Christ' eating bread and drinking wine at the last supper. This iconic language communicates above and beyond the literal meaning of the words; at its very best it communicates on an emotional and heartfelt level even before it is understood.

NEED TO KNOW

Know yourself

In order to create a language that works for mission amongst young people, we must first know our own language. We must take the time to become aware of what we say and how we explain things. If this is really difficult to do, then volunteer to help in a Sunday School class or with the mid-week children's work or even in a primary school. When we are forced to explain our faith to younger children, with their difficult questions, we become suddenly much more aware of the language that we use.

Know your community

All good missionaries need to know the community they are trying to reach! The young people we are trying to speak to may live only in the next street rather than the middle of South America but we still need to take time to know their language or even languages!

Know who talks best

God has given each of us different gifts and some people will be better at communicating than others. Find the people who are natural speakers both 'upfront' and in one to one communication. Find them and use them!

Know what we will lose

Language is a very powerful tool and if we begin to create a language that others can connect to they will begin to get involved. If we make our language accessible to others we must face the fact that potentially it will be changed by others and we will lose the power to control what is happening. This can leave us feeling very vulnerable.

Know when to shut up

My grandmother would say 'God gave you one mouth and two ears, there's a very good reason for that!' In all of the language creation, listening is probably the most important skill of all.

CASE STUDY: Words, words, words . . . all change!

The whole of this chapter is based on the idea that language changes. For most of us there is no need to think about the changes in language; they often happen slowly or else they are so distinctive they only affect the members of the group that use that language. Nouns, those words which give a name to something, like 'dog' or 'cat', really don't change very often. However, adjectives, that is words that describe, tend to change more frequently. The obvious example is the word 'gay', originally meaning 'carefree', which since the 1960s has gradually come to be a description of a homosexual male and has almost entirely lost its original meaning. In 2006 the word 'gay' gained yet another meaning: Chris Moyles on Radio 1 caused a great deal of conversation when he used the word 'gay' to mean rubbish or useless. Language is constantly evolving.

At the beginning of this chapter I explored a little the change in understanding about religious language. In the *Pocket Oxford Dictionary*, published in 1964, the definition of 'forgive' is 'pardon (me, my sin, me my sin), remit (the debt, him the debt.)'. The *Oxford Dictionary* of 1998, however, defines it as 'stop feeling angry or resentful towards (someone) for an offence, flaw, or mistake . . . used in polite expressions as a request to excuse or regard indulgently one's foibles, ignorance, or impoliteness: you will have to forgive my suspicious mind.' The first of these definitions gives a clear religious connotation to the word forgive, because it is intrinsically linked to sin, whereas 34 years later there is no mention of the word 'sin', and 'forgive' has become a polite way of saying 'ignore the foible I have made or am about to make'.

At this point you may be wondering what if anything this has to do with your youth group tomorrow night! These examples demonstrate how language can 'move' and come to mean different things to different people. At the most basic level the orange vegetable known as a 'swede' to some people is a turnip to others! Or another example is the word 'shoot', which can refer to a person attempting to score in football, injecting drugs or firing a gun! This illustrates both the excitement and the challenge of language as we begin to undertake 'mission and evangelism'.

So there is the theory but how does it work in practice? Here is an example. It is Lent. A group of young people have come together from two different areas; there are about twelve of them. Each week the group met and looked at a different aspect of faith including images of God, images of ourselves, issues of time. Each session involved games and some teaching, often through the sharing of stories; each session also involved some form of creativity. Young people were encouraged to write about their image of God, to re-create biblical passages such as the story of the Flood or of Creation. Each time, these young people struggled to find their own words to express ideas about God or the Bible. There was a great deal of conversation about what words were appropriate to use in church, and the youth workers had to take some risks as they encouraged the use of language which belonged to this group of young people, knowing that it could cause offence to the group of significantly older people who would be part of the congregation at

'There was a great deal of conversation about what words were appropriate to use in church, and the youth workers had to take some risks as they encouraged the use of language which belonged to this group of young people, knowing that it could cause offence to the group of significantly older people who would be part of the congregation at the Easter celebration.'

the Easter celebration. The young people were at first reticent to use their own language, preferring to hide behind the language they had learned; but those in the group who were not from church families had no learned 'church' language and so pushed the others to a more authentic expression of themselves. The end result of six weeks was an Easter dawn service in which most of the biblical material was rewritten in the language of this particular group. A sermon was delivered in the language which the leaders had learned with the group, although sadly the songs remained as they were and subsequently they were perhaps the least engaged-with part of the service.

THINKING IT THROUGH

So our language for mission must connect to young people. If it doesn't then it will be seen as 'superficial' or, worse still, 'artificial' and of no value. Creating a mission language cannot be done in an academic ivory tower.

What can we do to create opportunities for young people to be involved in creating mission language?

Our language must be inspired by the Holy Spirit who brings together God's people and equips them for mission. It is through the work of the Holy Spirit that we must create this mission language, allowing the Holy Spirit to enable the creation of a distinctive bridge that allows and even attracts others to walk across it into relationship with God and God's people.

Who are we trying to reach? What does their language sound like? Who can best help to build the bridge?

There is of course a problem with language; rather than being a bridge it is very easy for it to become a fence. Any language which is not accessible to others will act as a fence that prevents others from joining and maintains a sense of exclusivity. Language that is heavily poetic can do this, or language that is exclusively male dominated. Taking account of the instruction to call God 'Father' but ignoring the many stories of God being 'like' a mother or represented by the woman searching for the lost coin can be one example of such exclusive language. Exclusive language will keep people 'out' and therefore works against the sense of what it means to form a mission language.

What parts of our own language may act as a fence for others and so hinder mission?

As with all that we inherit, our language can be a blessing or a curse. There is a problem when our own religious language becomes so precious to us that we cannot let it go. We can become almost eaten up inside trying to keep our language from being tainted or touched by anyone else. It can become in many ways like the ring is for Gollum in *The Lord of the Rings* trilogy. Gollum strokes the ring and calls it 'my precious', never wanting anyone else to have it, and yet this attitude brought him to disaster.

The main question which we are left with after all of this is whether young people have to learn a new language or not. Is it necessary for them to learn traditional inherited words in order to express the Christian faith or can they begin to express their Christian faith in the words of their own language? This is a constant question for those involved in Bible translation. When the Bible is translated in a country that has no snakes, who does Eve talk to in the garden? If nobody in that country has ever seen a lamb, what do we do with Jesus the 'lamb of God'? There are stories of Bible translations where Satan is described as a creepy crawly or Jesus the 'piglet of God', because piglets, rather than lambs, had a special place in that society.

- Is it the actual words themselves that are most important and must therefore be preserved or is it the meaning that they convey?
- Are there particular words that you would find it very difficult if you were asked not to use them?
- Are there words that you would find difficult or offensive if others used them to express their faith?

Does all this really matter?

In asking if we need a new language we are exploring the tension between questions of Christian growth and assimilation. Do we require those new to the Christian faith to learn our language so that they can become exactly like us? Do young people need to change in order to fit in with the way we, the already gathered Church, are (assimilation), or do those new to faith change us because they bring new language, new experiences and new forms of expression? Perhaps their new language could encourage the existing

Church to understand afresh its faith and language rather than taking it for granted?

> 'Do we require those new to the Christian faith to learn our language so that they can become exactly like us? Do young people need to change in order to fit in with the way we, the already gathered Church, are (assimilation), or do those new to faith change us because they bring new language, new experiences and new forms of expression?'

The problem with any Christian language is that it may indeed be that actions and symbols are needed as well, because the words of the Christian gospel cannot be understood outside the experience of living faith.

SPEAKING IN TONGUES?

Language is power

Language is the power to form community and express yourself as an individual. We need language but it can also exclude.

Religious language

Is religious language being lost or just being 're-formed'? How much does it matter which one of these options is the case?

New generation = new challenges

With each new generation comes a different set of challenges, abilities and people. Does language need to change to reflect this?

Listen with both ears!

As Grandma would say, we have two ears and one mouth – it should tell you something!

SPEAKING IN TONGUES?

Books about language

J. L. Austin, *How to Do Things with Words*, Oxford University Press, 1962.

S. Blackburn, *Spreading the Word*, Clarendon Press, 1984.

T. Eagleton, *Literary Theory*, Blackwell, 1983.

M. Montgomery, *An Introduction to Language and Society*, Routledge, 1986.

Books about mission

D. J. Bosch, *Transforming Mission*, Orbis Books, 1991.

V. Donovan, *Christianity Rediscovered*, SCM Press, 1978.

L. Newbigin, *The Gospel in a Pluralist Society*, SPCK, 1989.

Sara Savage, Bob Mayo, Sylvia Collins-Mayo and Graham Cray, *Making Sense of Generation Y*, Church House Publishing, 2006.

P. Tillich, *Theology of Culture*, Oxford University Press, 1959.

Web resources

The Centre for Applied Linguistics (CAL) aims to promote and improve the teaching and learning of languages and to identify and solve problems related to language.
www.cal.org

Linguistics: An Introduction to Linguistics
www.geocities.com/CollegePark/3920

TAKING IT FURTHER

14 WHY DO YOUNG PEOPLE LEAVE?
Contemporary culture and Christian faith

Steve Hollinghurst

INTRODUCTION

The issue of young people leaving church is not new. What is new is that they are no longer likely to return. This seems to be caused by cultural changes that we need to address if young adults are to have Christian faith within our culture.

Church attendance statistics over the last 30 years show a distinct pattern.[1] There is higher than average childhood attendance, falling in the late teens and twenties with lowest attendance at about 25. Then people are increasingly likely to attend church as they get older: those over 65 are more likely to attend than children. This pattern is seen in countries with much higher church attendance[2] than Britain and seems likely to have been true 100 years ago too.[3]

THE ISSUE: Past the point of no return?

Some within the Church have been fooled into thinking that the pattern of the mid-twentieth century still holds. They have not been unduly alarmed when young people leave the Church, as they have expected them to return at significant moments in their lives – for example, to be married or to have children baptized. However, for reasons that will be explored below, this model no longer holds.

We should also note another major change in overall church attendance figures. In the early part of the twentieth century about 80 per cent of under-15s attended church or Sunday school regularly, but the figure now is only 20 per cent. If current teens and twenties who leave fail to return, by 2070 we can expect only 3 per cent of 80-year-olds, 3 per cent of children and 2 per cent of the population as a whole to be attending church. The 'Christendom system' has broken down.

We therefore need to develop a faith for post-Christendom that both enables young people in church to become Christian adults, and attracts young people with no church background to a similar faith.

BACKGROUND: The times they are a-changing

How are we to account for the fact that, in contrast to the pattern of the mid-twentieth century, young people who leave the Church today are unlikely to return in future?

To help us to understand this pattern, we need to look at the three 'cycles' which affect our lives. These are:

1. The relatively stable cycle of development over the life span, from birth to death, in which faith is challenged and must adapt to the issues raised at each life stage.
2. The 'generational cycle' that leads to changes over relatively small time periods and can sometimes be quite unstable (e.g. the shift from 'Generation X' to 'Generation Y').
3. A larger cycle of cultural shifts, in which there may be long periods of relative stability interspersed with periods of radical change (e.g the shift from modernity to postmodernity).

Let's look at how these operate in the lives of young people and how they impact on church attendance.

Developmental and generational shifts

The established pattern by which young people left church but often returned later in life may be the result of a particular stage of their development. The period from adolescence to early adulthood is one of questioning the received patterns of childhood and beginning to form one's own views and has often led to a time away from church.[4]

Within the generational cycles we are now talking about Generation Y teens and young adults, roughly those born in the 1980s and 1990s. If Generation X (born in the 1960s and 1970s) was seen as cynical and suspicious towards the world of their parents, Generation Y seems more hopeful and, it has been suggested, displays a more positive appreciation of family and social involvement.[5] A hundred years ago a shift like that from Generation X to Generation Y might be expected to mark a move towards an upswing in church attendance. Some US commentators have predicted this now for Generation Y there,[6] but there are no indications as yet of such a change. Indeed recent survey data of those in 18–24 age bracket would suggest that Generation Y is going to be even further from traditional religion and more open to alternative and occult views than Generation X.[7] If there is a generational issue it is more likely to be connected to the way Generation Y might express Christian faith, rather than their propensity to have Christian faith. In all of this the trends in church attendance and the survey results suggest that the key issue is the bigger cycle of cultural shift, in which we have shifted from modernity to postmodernity.

> 'The key issue is the bigger cycle of cultural shift, in which we have shifted from modernity to postmodernity.'

The big cycle shift from modernity to postmodernity
The big cycle shift is typified by what can be described as a move from modernity to postmodernity. How might this be impacting the lives of young people? There are a number of factors arising from this but behind many of them are three key elements: the triumph of consumerism, the experience of religious pluralism and a change in the way we decide what is true or right.[8] These mean that not only has our experience of the world changed but so has the way we understand that experience. It

> 'Not only has our experience of the world changed but so has the way we understand that experience.'

should also be noted that the roots of these changes can be traced back to the late nineteenth century, even if their major cultural impact has been seen only since the 1960s.

Contemporary consumerism has its roots in modernist capitalism, but it has made an important shift during the twentieth century. Advertising points the way by now selling us images rather than products. I don't simply buy a product – I buy the lifestyle the advertisement has said accompanies that product. For this reason the advertisement may tell me nothing about the product; it is the lifestyle that is being sold to me. At the same time manufacturers have shifted from supplying off-the-peg products, like Ford's Model T which consumers were famously told they could have in 'any colour you want as long as it's black', to creating designer products tailored to promote individual image and style.[9] If products have become statements of individual image and lifestyle, lifestyles and personal identities have become consumer commodities. This applies to values and beliefs as much as anything else. Religious faith becomes something I create to fit my lifestyle and image and meet my felt needs as a consumer. Such needs are likely to include a sense of what are 'good' ways of relating positively to the great diversity of people that make up our society and, increasingly, a positive response to environmental problems. However, the teachings of traditional religions will be expected to adapt to consumer demand and will not be seen as exclusive packages that can't be changed or stripped of attractive components to combine with bits from other religions or spiritual traditions.[10]

> **'Religious faith becomes something I create to fit my lifestyle and image and meet my felt needs as a consumer.'**

The increasing experience of religious pluralism following post-colonial immigration has reinforced consumerist trends in belief. This has led to a mushrooming of choice in the area of faith and spirituality and has also relativized individual religious positions. This all supports a move away from the concepts of identity prevalent in modernity which tended to emphasize our 'common humanity' and stressed that we were 'all really the same'.

A modernist liberal pluralism in which different religions are viewed as 'all really the same' has increasingly given way to a postmodern pluralism in which all are viewed as different but equally valid. This has allowed for greater consumer choice, enabling people to work out what is 'right for them' and thus celebrate their own individuality and diversity.

> 'A modernist liberal pluralism in which different religions are viewed as 'all really the same' has increasingly given way to a postmodern pluralism in which all are viewed as different but equally valid.'

At the same time, as a result of living alongside those of different religious positions and a suspicion of ultimate truth claims and superiority it has becoming increasingly difficult for people to feel confident that their religion 'has got it right'. This further decreases any sense that a religion offers a comprehensive and 'true' view of the world, and strengthens the sense that religious belief is something I choose as a consumer.

Changes in the understanding of 'truth' underpin these issues. In modernity, truth was seen as 'facts' and these were expressions of an underlying universal agreed reality. Facts were discovered through scientific experiment and reasoned rational argument. The universality of this concept of truth was reinforced by philosophical notions of a 'common rationality' shared by all humans, so the United States Declaration of Independence could say 'we hold these truths to be self evident'.[11] In a similar vein the reformers spoke of the 'plain meaning of Scripture'[12] and expected people to share a common mind about what that was. This understanding has increasingly been displaced for many by a concept of truth as based on experience and on how the individual, rather than anyone else, understands that experience. In such a world things can be 'true for me, but not for you'. If an underlying reality exists[13] it is probably unknowable and what knowledge we have is at best partial and subjective – the world as I see it is not the world as you see it. Films like the *Matrix* trilogy have helped popularize such ideas – what people thought was 'reality' turned out to be a computer program generating impulses in the brain. This critique of the notion that there are such things as 'facts' and a universal truth has been coupled with an awareness of the relationship between truth claims and power. Claiming to know what is true for somebody else is seen as an attempt to gain power over them. We no longer trust what experts tells us is true, but instead want to know their motives. In this way someone telling us the 'truth' about God is viewed with the same suspicion as a scientist telling us a food product is 'perfectly safe' to eat. On the other hand people are increasingly likely to value their own experience and opinion over that of experts. This is part of the reason why a book and film like *The Da Vinci Code* can do so well in spite of a whole welter of experts stepping up to attack its version of events – people simply find it more plausible or attractive than the expert opinion.

> **'We no longer trust what experts tells us is true, but instead want to know their motives. In this way someone telling us the "truth"about God is viewed with the same suspicion as a scientist telling us a food product is "perfectly safe" to eat.'**

Much of the way we do church and the culture of church in which young people learn the faith is still geared to a modernist worldview. Young people are often given 'the Christian truth' by 'Christian experts'. Church may offer little chance to participate as we stand, sit, kneel, sing and pray on the commands of leaders up front whom we face in rigid rows. The teaching comes in sermons delivered six feet above contradiction. All of this is so different from the world of the communities in which young people operate at school, online or the world of the media. The tension creates a feeling that Christian faith makes no sense of the world but instead can only be practised by those who shut themselves off from it. As was noted by Pete Ward,[14] the Church can collude in this separation by creating an entirely separate Christian youth subculture in order to 'keep them safe' from the temptations of non-church youth culture. This may seem to work for a time, but sooner or later young people will find it hard to avoid facing the culture of the world, which they are likely to do just at the time many have always dropped out of church. Viewed from the standpoint of a place where at last they can participate in culture, ask questions of authority and challenge their own received childhood opinions, church can seem very negative and stifling to a young person. A hundred years ago the world of church fitted the social fabric of Britain, and returning to church, perhaps to be married or to have children baptized, seemed natural. It no longer does so and to return to church seems to most like a bad mistake. Those who want to explore the spiritual are likely to be attracted to alternative spiritualities. The UK Pagan Federation[15] had to employ a youth officer for the first time in 2000 because of the vast number of enquiries they were getting from teenagers wanting to become witches and pagans.[16]

> 'Much of the way we do church and the culture of church in which young people learn the faith is still geared to a modernist worldview. Young people are often given "the Christian truth" by "Christian experts".'

It is also worth noting that while the majority will be shaped by an accommodation to contemporary culture a minority will be reacting against it. This results in a desire to find certainty in a culture that has rejected old certainties and indeed suggested there is nothing one can be certain about. It is for this reason that all religions are seeing a rise in conservative and fundamentalist groups.[17]

Key Points

Young people have always asked questions of faith, leading to some leaving church if only for a while. However, the basis on which these questions are asked has shifted. No longer are they necessarily seeking rational answers; rather they are often not seeking answers at all but a place in which they can live with the questions. Part of this process is a questioning of the authority of the Church, including the youth leader or minister. Also claims of 'absolute'

> **'Young people have always asked questions of faith, leading to some leaving church if only for a while. However the basis on which these questions are asked has shifted. No longer are they necessarily seeking rational answers, rather they are often not seeking answers at all but a place in which they can live with the questions.'**

truth will be seen as attempts at control and oppression. Most young people will not find it right to make decisions based on what someone else tells them is true or on the basis of unexamined citations of Scripture or church teaching. This goes against the tradition of most churches which, regardless of whether they are Evangelical, Catholic or Liberal, have developed strong authority structures that assume a modernist rational approach to faith. In contrast alternative spiritualities clearly are at home in the thought world young people inhabit. How should we respond to this thought world as it is expressed in the lives of young people around us?

CASE STUDY: The experience on the ground

Due to the way these issues often surface for young people in the late teens and early twenties, university ministry is an area which often has to face them. The story of one student related by a university chaplain is typical of many I and others have encountered.[18] This student was raised as a committed Christian within an evangelical youth group. When she came to university to study English she joined a thriving evangelical charismatic church with many student members and became active in the Christian Union, eventually becoming an executive officer. Increasingly she became aware that the questions asked of language and literature in her studies applied equally to the teachings of the Church and started to ask these questions. She quickly found that her faith and what she was being taught did not stand up to these questions and so began to pursue them with those in leadership within the church. The church offered firm answers to these questions, but these did not seem good to the student, who kept pushing for further and better answers. At this point the church deemed her a problem and sought to silence her. She concluded that her faith made no sense and began to talk of losing her faith. The university chaplaincy offered a connection to different streams of faith. Particularly notable was a retreat at Taizé in France. Part of such a retreat is a daily Bible study led by one of the brothers, a natural opportunity for this student to continue her searching questions, challenging the brother in the face of them to state 'How did he know he was right?' The brother thought for a while and responded 'Actually you may be right', deeply impressing the student. Added to this, Taizé offered meditation, silence and encounter with God in a way that was not about thought and debate. All of this started to build an approach to faith with which this student could go forward. Similar stories could also be told of young people coming from other traditions. I would add that having spent a number of years in inner city ministry as both youth evangelist and parish priest, people in those contexts also ask these kinds of questions, albeit with a different vocabulary and academic background, yet find they can engage with faith when they are encouraged to live with the unresolved doubts and try out the experience of Christian faith regardless.

THINKING IT THROUGH

- It may be helpful to reflect on how we deal with doubts and questions of faith. Is your response to seek and then hold to rational answers you feel can be relied on, or do you identify with the approach to doubts suggested here?
- Do you feel you are modernist or postmodernist in your approach to faith, or somewhere between?
- The relationship between faith and culture is difficult. Like Jesus we are called to incarnate faith in each generation and its culture. On the one hand we must not confuse the way our faith has adapted to culture in the past with the essence of faith. On the other, we must remain faithful to Christ and this will also involve a critical engagement with our culture. If your reaction to postmodern questions of faith is to attack the basis of those questions and seek ways to strengthen rational answers to faith as essential to Christianity, are you in fact not confusing Christianity

and modernity, and potentially choosing modernity instead of Christ?

■ If, however, you relish the thought of a faith that abandons all certainty and allows no-one to be considered an authority, and seek a faith based entirely on your own personal experience and inspiration, are you perhaps not properly discerning of the critique Christ might offer even as he was incarnate within a postmodern culture, just as he both affirmed and yet also challenged the world of his day?

How we live with these questions will be crucial to how we help young people in the Church to live with them.

WHY DO YOUNG PEOPLE LEAVE?

SUMMARY

It has always been the case that young people have left church; the real issue is why they no longer return. Postmodernity has accelerated the normal process whereby teens and early twenties often went through a period of questioning faith as they sought to form 'adult' views of their own. If once it was normal for many to return to a self-professed faith, now few do so. This is because modern churches, their practices and presentation of faith make little sense to postmodern young adults. The exception is the minority who seek a place of security and certainty as a refuge from contemporary culture at least in some areas. This bolsters a Christian youth subculture that becomes increasingly conservative and thus even further removed from the majority of young people, including most of the minority who have a Christian upbringing, who are likely to turn away from Christianity, and the majority who have no history of Christian faith. This situation can create the false impression that 'what works' is a conservative youth ministry, an impression that further bolsters an exclusive pitch to the reactionary minority in our culture. We need to develop youth outreach and discipleship that can reach the majority who fully embrace postmodernity, yet also try to care for those who are in reaction against it. It would be hoped that this might be possible in one ministry, but it may simply be too much to ask for. It may well be that conservative and postmodern approaches will need to be developed as parallel tracks. If so, my prayer is that this can be done with generosity and not judgementalism: both approaches are needed in faithfulness to God in this day and age.

An effective approach to such ministry is, I think, to embrace rather than suppress the questioning of received doctrine, and to encourage an approach to spirituality and faith that is also non-rational.[19] Only by doing this can young people develop a faith that not only is happy to stand alongside other faiths and still feel confident in Christianity, but is also happy with the internal doubts and questions that arise within the believer. In the past, questions from without and doubts from within were tackled with a rationalist apologetic that had a supposedly water-tight answer to every question. This approach has been found severely wanting in today's world – people know that the answers are not so certain and that many Christians believe different things which can be shown to be consistent with the Christian tradition. The faith they need is one that often says 'I'm not sure, but it might be like this' rather than 'This is the Christian answer'. They will also need a faith that is rooted in an audiovisual culture and in which God is experienced rather than thought about; indeed in which we admit, with the early church tradition, that God cannot be fully under-stood and that this is at the heart of faith.[20]

Alan Jamieson's books *A Churchless Faith* (SPCK, 2002) and *Journeying in Faith* (SPCK, 2004) may primarily focus on 30-somethings plus, but the issues he relates to are those of people struggling very often with postmodernity and church. These are well worth studying to reflect further on the issues facing young people. That this is so further enforces the suggestion that these issues are not primarily about age or generation but a large-scale culture shift.

Richter and Francis, *Gone but not Forgotten* (Darton, Longman & Todd, 1998) is again looking at those across the generations who are church leavers, but offers useful insights (although unfortunately it is now out of print).

Sara Savage, Bob Mayo, Sylvia Collins-Mayo and Graham Cray, *Making Sense of Generation Y* (Church House Publishing, 2006) has useful discussions on a number of issues relating to this generation.

Phil Rankin, *Buried Spirituality* (Sarum College Press, 2006) offers further useful insights on Generation Y approaches to church and spirituality.

Finally, in addition to sources cited in my footnotes, I would recommend Gibbs and Bolger, *Emerging Churches* (Baker Academic, 2005). This gives voice to those in the alternative/emerging church scene, young adults in the main struggling with faith in postmodernity; many of them have left church as they knew it but found a way to remain within the faith.

POSTSCRIPT: Why mission alone isn't the answer

David Booker

Congratulations, you have made it to the end of the book, or at least flicked through and settled upon this bit to read! Assuming you have read the book, you have now thought about a whole array of missiological principles and possibilities. Everything from equipping young people to share their faith to working in schools, from examining the language we use to understanding that mission informs our care for the environment and the poor. You might think that if you are not ready for mission with young people now, you never will be. If only it were that simple!

Those who work with young people are working in a constantly shifting environment. We can respond, but we cannot dictate how that environment evolves or how it will influence our ability to work with God in mission among young people. The chapters of this book have explored some of the current opportunities and issues we face in youth mission. This postscript will outline three concerns that those who engage with young people must continually live with as they seek to work:

1. How can we appropriately read our cultures and engage in mission in ways that respond to them?
2. How do we live with the fact that the church's culture is very often alien to the world around us and to the young people we work with?
3. How do we live with the fact that there is no scientific formula for success in mission and that the visible results do not always match the effort we make?

Throughout this book the writers have acknowledged the rapidly changing world in which we, and the young people we work with, live. As the world changes our challenge is to reshape our approach and find appropriate new ways of building bridges into the world of young people. However, too often our knee-jerk response is to reject contemporary culture rather than see within it new opportunities to engage the world. Perhaps the best recent example of sections of the Church getting it wrong is the negative response to *Jerry Springer the Opera*. I believe the protest that surrounded *Springer* was

> **'As the world changes our challenge is to reshape our approach and find appropriate new ways of building bridges into the world of young people. However, too often our knee-jerk response is to reject contemporary culture rather than see within it new opportunities to engage the world.'**

an almost perfect example of how to miss a missiological opportunity offered to us by contemporary culture and put people off the Church in the process.

In case you spent the last few years on Mars, here is a quick history lesson. February 2001 saw Richard Thomas performing a work in progress called *How to write an opera about Jerry Springer*. In August 2002 *Jerry Springer the Opera* was a sell-out hit at the Edinburgh Festival, and then in April 2003 it had a sell-out run at the National Theatre in London. 2004 saw it open in the West End, where it then won just about every major theatre award going. As a result the BBC decided to show the musical but were met by a passionate campaign from some Christian pressure groups, culminating in over 47,000 complaints being received ahead of the broadcast – an all-time record. Most of the complaints focused on the show's portrayals of Jesus, God and Mary, and the free use of four-letter words. Despite the complaints, the BBC went ahead with the broadcast and the show attracted an audience of 1.8 million people. Then 2006 saw an extensive tour of the show across the UK, where it was met in many locations by groups of Christians standing outside protesting at what they saw as the blasphemous content and persistent bad language.

I know, and value the opinions of, a number of Christian friends who were deeply concerned about the show. However, I believe not only that the response of the protesters was wrong in the message it sent out, but also that we missed a golden opportunity to use the show to engage with the many young people who were moved by its themes. As I left the theatre I found the presence of the protesters to be both misplaced and embarrassing for at least three reasons.

First, although some high-profile Christian commentators questioned the play's quality, *Jerry Springer the Opera* is widely recognized as a serious piece of theatre with genuine artistic merit, which raises issues and questions about the nature of our society and the media. Major theatrical awards are not presented on the basis of blasphemous content or swearing but on the perceived quality, entertainment and value of the show. Just because some Christians may not like *Springer*, or disagree with its message, it is not a good enough reason to write it off. As a serious work of art it deserves serious debate and consideration rather than shouting down.

> **'Just because some Christians may not like *Springer*, or disagree with its message, it is not a good enough reason to write it off. As a serious work of art it deserves serious debate and consideration rather than shouting down.'**

Secondly, I passionately believe in freedom of speech. That means that other people must have a right to challenge or offend me, to make me think and to show me other ways of seeing things. That may be an uncomfortable experience for me, but if I want the right to speak to and disagree with others, then other people must be allowed to have that right too. I do not personally believe that God needs protection from any law, but freedom of speech is essential to allow evangelism to flourish. If we attack freedom of speech there is a real danger we inadvertently limit our own freedom to witness.

Thirdly, I believe effective mission begins with listening to our culture. Any approach that simply condemns the play or those who enjoy it is counter-productive, more likely to distance people from the gospel than attract them to it. My own local paper carried a number of letters from concerned Christians that gave the impression that the Christian community would be rubbing their hands in glee because those who saw the play would burn in hell for doing so. If we are motivated to mission by love we will begin by listening, not condemning.

If we do take the time to listen and explore some of the issues the play raises we might be surprised by what we find. Let me give you three examples of ways in which the play might have something to say to our work with young people, examples of how much contemporary culture presents us with opportunities for engagement.

The first half of the play sees a number of guests appearing on the 'Jerry Springer Show' to share their secrets with loved ones. Although they exhibit various types of bizarre and selfish behaviour, beneath their revelations is a desperate desire to be loved and accepted for who they are. One guest powerfully sings the words:

> I'm tired of failing, I'm tired of all this trying,
> I want to do some living, I've had enough of dying.

She sums up a real cry from Jerry's guests for something 'more', that life as they know it cannot be all that is meant to be. Augustine recognized the same human disease, claiming that our hearts are restless until they find their rest in God. Just maybe one of the reasons that *Jerry Springer the Opera* is so successful is that many people seeing the play recognize that same dissatisfaction with life. Despite all the goods and freedoms our postmodern society offers, there is still a longing for 'life in all its fullness' that can only be met in God. *Springer* reminds us that while people may look for fullness of life in sex or fame or relationships, they on their own cannot bring fulfilment. We might call this a recognition of spiritual hunger, but the show reminds us that few even consider looking for such fulfilment in church. We are not so much deliberately rejected as simply irrelevant to most people looking for meaning to their lives.

> **'Despite all the goods and freedoms our postmodern society offers, there is still a longing for "life in all its fullness" that can only be met in God. *Springer* reminds us that while people may look for fullness of life in sex or fame or relationships, they on their own cannot bring fulfilment.'**

The second half of the show is a hallucination, taking place in Jerry's mind following his shooting by a guest on the show. In this dream he imagines being called to reconcile heaven and hell in a special show held at Satan's request. The guests on the show sing a song asking the Jesus character where he was in their times of need. These times range from the banal ('Where were you when the keys were lost?') to the tragic ('Where were you when the children died?'). As they sing their questions Springer's Jesus responds by asking where his listeners were when he was crucified. Satan in turn asks, 'Always on about the crucifixion, that was 2,000 years ago, why don't you get over it?'

That profound scene says a great deal about the way the churches' outreach is often perceived. Too often in our mission and evangelism we don't seem to listen; too often we seem to ignore difficult questions. Many people do wonder what all the fuss is about a man dying 2,000 years ago and how that can have any relevance to their life today. Simply continually shouting that the cross does have relevance, without exploring why or how, is no help at all to those who don't understand. Failure to understand the cross is not a new problem of course; the apostle Paul called it 'foolishness' to those who didn't understand. The question this scene poses for Christians is how do we listen and make ourselves heard in our ever-changing culture? I find it sadly ironic that many of the protests against the show have exactly mirrored this scene – unwilling to listen, arrogant and ignoring the humanity of those on the other side of the fence. I couldn't help but feel ashamed at how well that particular scene presented the way we Christians often communicate, as personified by many of those I saw outside the theatre doors. I saw the show in two locations and on both occasions had protesters shoving leaflets into

> 'Many people do wonder what all the fuss is about a man dying 2,000 years ago and how that can have any relevance to their life today. Simply continually shouting that the cross does have relevance, without exploring why or how, is no help at all to those who don't understand.'

my hand without attempting to make any connection with me as a person. The impression they left me with was that they were cross and disappointed with me, not that they loved me!

As well as being both shocking and funny, *Jerry Springer the Opera* satirizes and questions the type of potentially exploitative television programme on which it is based. It asks why people put themselves in the spotlight for their few minutes of fame and why people want to watch. The answers it suggests are not flattering. The play exposes the way we often gain a sense of self worth by comparing ourselves with others. Look at them, we say to ourselves, I am not as bad as them so I must be okay. This is of course far from a Christian outlook, but it is one we often fall into. Jesus told the parable of the Pharisee and the tax collector. The Pharisee proudly stood in the temple and thanked God he was not like other men, but was holy and righteous. The tax collector threw himself on God's mercy and begged to be forgiven his sins. As they left the temple only the tax collector was right with God. I would argue that one of the themes of the play is that we really are all the same despite the exploitative nature of many confessional television programmes. All a mix of pain and hope, selfishness and fear, and therefore none of us is in a position to judge. We are all fragile and all seek to be loved.

So here is a funny, powerful, moving play that asks questions about what it means to be human, that can shed uncomfortable light on how the world sees the Church and that challenges those who see themselves as morally superior. It is a play that stops me sitting comfortably and makes me ask questions of myself because of far more than its four letter words. Yes, it has lots of language I'd rather was not there and no, I do not recognize the Jesus presented to us in Jerry Springer's dream as the Jesus who is my Lord and Saviour. But then I live every day with people who have radically different understandings of who Jesus is. I'm happy to chat and discuss with them; I don't want to ban them from speaking.

What message did the protesters leave people with as they left the theatre? Probably that God is grumpy and that he disapproves of them, a message a long way from the picture of God we want people to have. I know those people meant well and had prayed hard before they acted but I really don't think they knew the impression they were giving. To be effective in evangelism and mission we must listen to what our culture is saying to us, not simply drown out its voice by preaching more loudly. I'm not embarrassed by evangelism, but I certainly find some evangelism embarrassing!

> 'To be effective in evangelism and mission we must listen to what our culture is saying to us, not simply drown out its voice by preaching more loudly. I'm not embarrassed by evangelism, but I certainly find some evangelism embarrassing!'

Those who work with young people have the dangerous task of stepping out of the comfy Christian box to try and make sense of faith in the world of young people. I would argue that if we want to be taken seriously we should listen and ask more questions before daring to condemn; otherwise we might miss the next golden opportunity to come, in just the same way the opportunity presented by *Springer* was missed. Reading a culture is not simple, but if we want to root the faith of our young people in their world we have no choice but to try. After all, Jesus came not to condemn the world, despite what some of his representatives may lead us to think!

DANGER – TOXIC CHURCH!

How do we live with the fact that the Church's culture is very often alien to the world around us and to the young people we work with?

Misreading our culture and misusing opportunities to communicate to young people through it is a real problem. However, even if we engage well and 'do mission' perfectly there is another great problem lurking in the wings: the Church.

We need to be clear from the start that the Church is greatly loved by God and is crucial to our health if we want to grow as Christians. Having said that, a large 'but' must be added because anyone who has been a church member for any length of time will know that it is rarely, if ever, what it could or should be. At one level we need to be gracious and accept that those of us who call ourselves Christians are also imperfect, not living up to our high calling. However, unless we recognize that the Church is sick we are unlikely to be able to take the steps necessary to begin fixing it so that we are better able to reach young people in mission.

Deep-frozen babies

When a baby is born it needs care, food and warmth to grow and develop healthily. We know very well that putting a newborn baby into a deep freeze and expecting it to thrive is plain stupid. Yet if part of mission to young people is seeing them come to faith and grow in it, why do we effectively do that very thing to them? It is of course not simply that a lot of our churches have poor heating arrangements. The way we are church is deeply alien to the lives of most young people. Alison Booker showed how our language can be deeply problematic in communicating with young people, but our music, dress codes, images and tea in green cups can all be equally problematic.

I once saw a young man walk into my current church's morning service. He was greeted and welcomed at the door and then handed the hymnbook, service sheet and week's newsletter. He looked down at the items given to him and politely handed them back. 'Sorry,' he said, 'I don't read very well.' He walked back out of the church door and I have never seen him again.

Even those churches we might see as accessible have many hidden barriers that those of us who know church find hard to recognize. Many of our services are still deeply influenced by the way the Victorians worshipped, rather than being based on today's world. Why should a young person need to be able to worship like a Victorian in order to meet with God? If the word becoming flesh means anything to us, it means we cannot demand that young people adopt our culture in order to worship God.

Much of the way we do church today simply does not work, even for those who lead it. I have been amazed by the number of church leaders who have told me that they could not cope with being a member of their own church, and would worship elsewhere, if they were not the leader. So many of those who sit in our pews are there because they know as good Christians they should be there rather than because church 'works' for them. However, while older generations remain largely loyal to the Church because of what it could be, young people's culture sees them very willing to get rid of what does not work. Young people will not come to church because they should, but because they meet with God there and belong to a living, caring community. Perhaps the willingness of young people to leave even does us a favour? They are honest enough not to just go through the motions of churchgoing but to demand a church that works. So many older people in our pews share that desire for a church that feeds their faith and equips them to live out God's mission in the world, and are equally frustrated. We will never get that church we hope for if we don't admit that the one we currently have is often culturally a deep freeze.

This does not mean that we can simply leap on the latest church trend and copy what works down the road. It is a question of how we decide what church, in its widest sense, should be like. Most of the time the style of any given church is fixed, whether traditional, alternative, or contemporary. Those who come into the church come on the basis that that is what it is like. However, what if, rather than seeing a church's way of operating as fixed, we understood that a church should flexibly adapt to be suitable to those in and around it, asking what shape it needs to adopt to best serve those who are its members and potential members?

Those who work with young people have a real responsibility to help the church adapt, even if they don't always feel that their support for change is welcome. Some youth workers use their contact with young people to escape the Church's cultural deep freeze and do things with the young people that make more sense to them than traditional church. This might be a good survival instinct on the part of the individual youth worker, but it won't raise the Church's temperature or make it more outward-looking. Youth workers need not only to focus on the young people they serve, but also to be advocates for change in the wider church so that young people can feel welcomed and accepted there without needing to learn a new culture first.

> 'Youth workers need not only to focus on the young people they serve, but also to be advocates for change in the wider church so that young people can feel welcomed and accepted there without needing to learn a new culture first.'

THE MYSTERY OF YOUTH MINISTRY

How do we live with the fact that there is no scientific formula for success in mission and the visible results do not always match the effort we make?

We could spend a long time lamenting the failure of the Church and the difficulties of discerning cultural opportunities for sharing the gospel. Throw into the mix the frustration of working with unreliable young people and the often shameful way the Church treats those who work with young people, be they employed or not, and we could soon convince ourselves to give up. However, there are two mysterious truths, or laws in youth ministry that can give us hope, or at least stop us feeling personally responsible for our success or failure.

The two mysterious laws of youth ministry:

- The wind blows where it will.
- Youth work that doesn't change the worker will never change the youth!

The wind blows where it will

Ability and hard work plus understanding and resources plus prayer and good looks do not guarantee results! The problem with a book like this is that it can lead to the assumption that you only need to do things in the right way for them to work. Obviously we want to do things well not badly, safely not with undue risks, and relevantly not boringly. However, knowing how to do things, having the resources and team and working yourself into the ground do not guarantee results. The truth is that even when we seem to do everything right there are times when nothing seems to result from it. We may know in our heads that we are called to faithfulness not success, but in a world where success matters it can be hard not to judge ourselves against others.

The culture of the quick-fix solution is alive both outside and inside the Church. Using a particular prayer, following a particular resource or adopting a particular style of approach might lead to visible results, or it might not. Believing there is a single answer to fix our problems if only we can find it can be a recipe for disaster, leaving us feeling frustrated and disillusioned because our ministry with young people isn't as successful as we would like. Sometimes we work and pray our socks off and nothing seems to happen. Like those in the 400-year period between the Old and New Testaments, we have to be faithful anyway and trust that God is still working his purpose out in the way he sees fit even if little seems to be happening. There was nothing wrong with the people of that period that had to be fixed before God could move. It was simply that God in his wisdom decided not to send Jesus until he knew the time was right. Seeds take time to grow. Just because we have yet to see them break the surface does not mean that the harvest has failed, just that we must wait.

How do we respond when the work is hard and no progress seems to be being made? Do we find someone to blame? Perhaps the young people themselves? Their parents' lack of commitment or unrealistic demands? The wider Church and its lack of support for what we are doing? Or even maybe ourselves, wondering if we should give up? There is no quick fix when working with young people and often the results seem unfair. We need to learn from those who see success in their ministries, but we need to remember that they are graciously blessed, not in possession of a magic wand that will work in every situation. We cannot make God work on demand just because he has done something elsewhere; we simply need to keep faithful where we are called to be. After all, the wind blows where it will and we cannot control or tame it.

> **'We cannot make God work on demand just because he has done something elsewhere, we simply need to keep faithful where we are called to be. After all, the wind blows where it will and we cannot control or tame it.'**

Youth work that doesn't change the worker will never change the youth!

What are young people looking for? Exciting programmes? Good-looking leaders? Inspiring worship? Opportunities to serve others? Maybe all of those things are on the wish list somewhere, but what is top? I believe young people are looking for two things, significance and love. Whether they are able to articulate their need for significance and love or not, it is the search for these things that drives much of what they do and how they act.

As those who work with young people we may not be able to offer the trendiest activities or the most contemporary worship. There will always be other, better-resourced and advertised forms of entertainment for young people to attend. However, what we can offer is unconditional love, both our love as leaders and of course God's love that motivates ours. If young people are genuinely loved they will believe they are significant, that they matter. But love is costly. Turning up to play table tennis for an hour a week is not what is needed. Instead we need to really connect, to be open and share, to answer questions and be willing to be challenged ourselves. Genuine relationship is about both partners changing and growing in response to the other. As a parent I learn a huge amount about myself through interacting with my children. If youth work is something we do only *for* young people and not also *with* them, we have missed the point. Christian youth ministry brings a unique perspective; for us, young people are not our clients or customers but our fellow disciples, walking the same road as us. A 'do it for them' mentality is much safer but never allows young people to develop their own gifts and become responsible; instead it builds a wall between worker and young person.

> 'Christian youth ministry brings a unique perspective; for us, young people are not our clients or customers but our fellow disciples, walking the same road as us.'

Youth leaders who are open and willing to learn from their interactions with young people as well as teach them are those who will tend to see results. Youth workers who take a superior attitude never encourage openness, honesty and real change in young people's lives. If we are not willing to be changed by our young people we will never see them change.

SIMPLE BUT COSTLY

You may find this hard to believe, but the longer I have been involved in youth ministry, the more books I have read, courses I have attended and training I have delivered, the simpler I believe working with young people is. At the heart of our mission to young people is this question: how do we show young people we love them? All the ideas, games and strategies in the world are wasted unless love for young people is at the heart of our action. How will they know God's love unless they experience it through us? If you want to engage effectively in mission to and with young people only one thing is really required. That we love them.

How do we know God loves us? Through seeing that love in others and ultimately in the life of his son Jesus Christ. But here is the problem: love is simple, but it is also terribly costly for those who have it. The love of Christ for you and me led him to the cross. If we are committed to following him we may find our love for young people drawing us to uncomfortable places too. Jesus' mission led him to pain, heartbreak and regular misunder-standing. As we follow him in mission to young people we should expect no less.

What drove Jesus on was his love for each one of us and his knowledge of what he was accomplishing for us. By his pain we were set free from all that held us back and were reconciled to God. Now as those reconciled we are called to join in God's mission. It will be hard, frustrating and painful, we will be let down and disappointed, but there is nothing like seeing young people discovering God's love for themselves and recognizing their potential as being made in God's image. It is a tremendous privilege to be called to mission with and to young people. As we follow that call we too will find ourselves continually transformed by God's grace. Each writer in this book would testify to the fact that true mission is not only something we do, but something that changes us in the process of doing it. Mission is our calling and our privilege; we may never fully understand it, but we know that as we step out in mission with God he not only transforms our world, but also transforms our own hearts in the process.

> 'We are called to join in God's mission. It will be hard, frustrating and painful, we will be let down and disappointed, but there is nothing like seeing young people discovering God's love for themselves and recognizing their potential as being made in God's image.'

Perhaps then there are three reasons for continuing in mission: God's call, the need of the world, and our own benefit. How typically gracious of God that mission is not only a job that he gives us but also a means of transforming us into the people he created us to be. If we love God, love our young neighbours, and want to be all God intends us to be, then mission is the key.

With so many opportunities and needs in the lives of young people, what are we waiting for? God is already doing his mission; let's try and keep up with him!

> 'With so many opportunities and needs in the lives of young people, what are we waiting for? God is already doing his mission; let's try and keep up with him!'

NOTES

2 Naturally speaking

1. *Youthwork* magazine, January 2006.

4 Starting from scratch

1. Editor's note: When I first arrived as Youth Adviser for the Leicester Diocese I surveyed the parishes and found that fewer than 40 per cent had any form of ongoing contact with young people aged 14–25. All the national statistics point to a continued decline in the coming years, although Church of England statistics show an increase in the numbers of children and young people attending over the last two years (see Church of England statistics at www.cofe.anglican.org/info/statistics and also www.christian-research.org.uk

6 Class act

1. P. Brierley, *Steps to the Future Christian Research*, Scripture Union, 2000, p. 48 (but see also note about Church of England statistics in Ch. 4).
2. E. Williams, *The Schools Work Handbook*, Scripture Union, 1996, p. 14.
3. Education Reform Act 1988, HMSO, 1988, para. 1 of section 2 a), quoted in Williams, *Handbook*, p. 47.
4. Department For Education Circular No. 1/94, para. 16, quoted in Williams, *Handbook*, p. 47.
5. Education Reform Act 1988, HMSO, 1988, para. 7, section 1, quoted in Williams, *Handbook*, p. 48.
6. See QCA web site, www.qca.org.uk
7. See www.teachernet.gov.uk/wholeschool/extendedschools
8. Laughton Deanery Schools Worker Trust Constitution 1997, p. 11.
9. Williams, *Handbook*, p. 53.
10. M. Robinson, *The Faith of the Unbeliever*, Monarch, 1994, pp. 135–6.

8 Ignorance is bliss?

1. More information can be found at http://www.cofe.anglican.org/info/interfaith/

9 Feeling the heat

1. Writing in the journal *Science* on 9 January 2004.
2. More information can be found at www.wmo.ch

3. More information can be found at
   www.conservation.org/xp/CIWEB/programs/climatechange
4. ACC–8, p.101.
5. www.shrinkingthefootprint.cofe.anglican.org

11   Mission as package holiday?

1. See www.merseyfest.com
2. See www.b-cent.com
3. www.soulaction.org/Opportunities_and_Events/Durban.htm
4. D. J. Bosch, *Transforming Mission: Paradigm shifts in theology of mission*, Orbis Books, 1991, p. 9.
5. Bosch, *Transforming Mission*, pp. 298–302.
6. This is not a ubiquitous position. There are good examples where missionaries specifically countered and challenged the injustices of colonialism. See. P. Sampson, 'Cross purposes' in *Third Way* 22 (5) (June 1999), pp. 23–5.
7. See for example J. A. Kirk, *What is Mission? Theological Explorations*, Darton, Longman & Todd, 1999, especially pp. 75–95.
8. D. MacCannell, *The Tourist: A new theory of the leisure class*, University of California Press, 1999 (first published in 1976).
9. J. Jafari, 'Tourism models: The sociocultural aspects', *Tourism Management* (June 1987), pp. 151–9.
10. Young people who go on short-term mission trips, in the same ways as those who go 'travelling' for a short time are also a type of tourist. There is some specific writing on the phenomenon of western young people going 'travelling' which also serves to inform why Christian young people may take gap years for similar reasons. See L. Desforges, 'Checking out the planet: Global representations/local identities and youth travel', in Skelton and Valentine, *Cool Places: Geographies of youth cultures*, Routledge, 1998.
11. See for example P. Pattullo and M. Manley, *Last Resorts: The cost of tourism in the Caribbean*, Cassell, 1996.
12. In addition, music acts and worship reflected the urban multi-cultural context of London in the tent city sites.
13. The staging of experiences specifically for tourists is a recognized feature of package (and other) holidays. I discuss this in more detail in my expanded paper on this topic.

14. This process was not without difficulty, however – assigning people to projects was complex and resulted in some projects getting double or less than half the expected numbers on some days.
15. Conversations and incidents I recorded in field notes.
16. Discussed explicitly in L. Newbigin, *The Gospel in a Pluralist Society*, SPCK, 1989.
17. EA/Shaftsbury Society, *SITC Evaluation Report* 2004, pp. 19–20.

12   Church hall vs. lychgate

1. A lychgate is a covered gate at the boundary of a churchyard traditionally used by pall bearers to rest the coffin on the way to burial.
2. Greek word, often translated as 'repent', which literally means 'to turn around'.

13   Speaking in tongues?

1. Douglas Coupland, *Generation X*, St Martin's, 1991, p. 126.
2. Sara Savage, Bob Mayo, Sylvia Collins-Mayo and Graham Cray, *Making Sense of Generation Y*, Church House Publishing, 2006, p. 21.
3. Janssen, De Hart and Gerardts, cited in Savage et al, *Generation Y*, p. 21.
4. T. Eagleton, *Literary Theory*, Blackwell, 1983, p. 64.
5. Cited in M. Montgomery, *An Introduction to Language and Society*, Routledge, 1986, p. 190.
6. Lecture in Sheffield Diocese, 14 November 2000.
7. D. J. Bosch, *Transforming Mission*, Orbis Books, 1991, p. 412.
8. Pat Lynch, *Awakening the Giant*, Darton, Longman & Todd, 1990, p. 10.
9. Cited in Montgomery, *Introduction to Language*, p. 190.

14   Why do young people leave?

1. See *Religious Trends* 5, Christian Research Association, 2005.
2. The USA is a good example in spite of its higher overall church attendance. See data online from the Association of Religious Data Archives at www.thearda.com
3. See Robin Gill, *The Myth of the Empty Church*, SPCK, 1993, pp. 301, 318.
4. See James W. Fowler, *Stages of Faith*, Harper & Row, 1981; also survey material at www.childtrends.org as cited at http://www.washtimes.com/national/20050412–121457–4149r.htm

(*Washington Times* article, 12 April 2005); also material at http://www.search-institute.org

5. Cf. discussion of the 'happy midi-narrative' in Savage et al, *Making sense of Generation Y*, p. 35ff.

6. See Winkie Pratney, *Fire on the Horizon: How the revival generation will change the world*, Gospel Light Publishing, 1999.

7. See the Populus 'Morals, ethics and religion survey', April 2005 and the ICM 'Faith' poll November 2005.

8. To read further on such areas of postmodernity, see R. Lundin, *The Culture of Interpretation*, Eerdmanns, 1993; J. R. Middleton and B. J. Walsh, *Truth is Stranger than it Used to Be*, IVP, 1993; Zygmunt Bauman, *Liquid Modernity*, Polity Press, 2000.

9. See Zygmunt Bauman, *Liquid Modernity*.

10. See Nick Spencer, *Beyond Belief*, LICC, 2003.

11. 4 July 1776, opening sentence of second paragraph.

12. The point is argued by Martin Luther, *Lectures on Galatians* (1519) and *Lectures on Galatians* (1535). These are published in *Luther's Works*, ed. Jaroslav Pelikan and Helmut T. Lehmann, 55 vols, St. Louis: Concordia; Philadelphia: Muhlenberg, 1955–76, as volumes 26 and 27. Calvin argued for the same point. See Calvin, *Institutes of the Christian Religion* 2:925, ed. John T. McNeill, Westminster Press, 1960; J. Calvin, *Genesis*, 1554; Banner of Truth, 1984.

13. And at the hard end of postmodern philosophy some will argue that the world is simply a projection of our own minds.

14. Pete Ward, *Growing up Evangelical: Youthwork and the making of a subculture*, SPCK, 1996.

15. www.paganfed.org

16. This interest has helped spawn the highly successful and youth orientated Witchfest, run by the Children of Artemis www.witchraft.org

17. See Gilles Keppel, *The Revenge of God*, Polity Press, 1994.

18. I was a university chaplain myself between 1999 and 2003.

19. I do not mean irrational!

20. See Hebrews 11.1. This strand of theology has been preserved within the Orthodox tradition, which has used both a multiplicity of descriptions for God and also a silence about God that acknowledges that all we say is in fact inaccurate.